How to Get Unstuck and Live Your Best Life 2 books in 1

Ikigai, How to Choose your Career Path and Discover Your Strengths +
Your Unlimited Opportunities & the Art of Personal Transformation

Clement Harrison

Your Free Gift

Want to finally turn your passion into profit and gain access to a roadmap on how to build your online store successfully?

Whether you decide to monetize your passion on the side or build a real business from what you love, you'll inevitably need an online presence.

I'd like to give you a gift as my way of saying thanks for purchasing this book. It's my 20-page PDF Action guide titled *The Online Store Game Plan: 8 Simple Steps to Create Your Profitable Online Business*

It's short enough to read quickly, but meaty enough to know the actionable steps to take when starting your online business

In *The Online Store Game Plan* you'll discover:

- How to create your online store in 8 simple steps
- 3 key pillars that will lay the foundations of your online success
- The perfect online business model for your company
- What online platform will suit your business
- Several ways to attract customers to your online store

And much more....

Scan the QR-Code Now to access *The Online Store Game Plan* and set yourself up for online success!

Table of Contents

Ikigai, How to Choose your Career Path and Discover Your Strengths

Introduction 11
Chapter 1: Assessing Your Current Situation 15
    Analyzing Your Current Position 18
    Signs That You May Need a Change: 28
Chapter 2: Finding Your Way 35
    Are You Stuck or In Limbo? 35
    Discovering WHY? 36
    Changing Careers 39
    Analyze Yourself 40
    Analyze Your Role 41
    Discovering Your Ikigai 43
    Further Career Considerations 46
    Leaving Change Too Late 46
    Be Clear On What You Want 49
    Let's Talk Money... 51
    Finding My Strengths 52
Chapter 3: Exploring Alternative Careers 55
    Online Assessments 55
    Be Realistic in Your Expectations 56
    Investigating the Unknown 57
    Network or Attend Conferences 59
    Look at Pay Scales 59
    Career Prospects or Not? 60
    The Information Technology Age: A Case Study 61

    Can I Afford to Step Back into an Entry
Level Position?.. 63
    Do I Need Any New Skills?................................. 63
    Do Your Research 64
    Find A Way to Showcase Your New Skills 64
    Consider Your V.I.P.S... 65
    Put A Plan Together.. 67
    Is This Really What You Want? 68

Chapter 4: Improving Your Skills............. 71
    Identify Why You Really Want to Move 71
    How To Identify Your Skills 73
    Evaluate Your Current Skill Set 73
    How Do You Go About Developing New
Skills? 76
    Do You Need Further Studies?...........................77
    Other Ways To Improve Your Current Skills... 79
    Setting SMART Goals 80
    Other Access to Knowledge 81
    Skills Every Company Needs............................. 82

**Chapter 5: What Can You Still Do While
In Your Job? 85**
    Consider Remaining In The Same Industry 85
    Repair Relationships Before Moving 86
    Proactive Things to Do 87
    What You Should Do NOW 89
    Keep A Record of Accomplishments................ 90
    Connect with Colleagues on Social Media 91
    Do Your Job Well.. 91
    Appoint an Accountant...................................... 92
    Consider Roadblocks... 93

Chapter 6: Finding The Opportunities..... 96
    Updating Your Resume and Cover Letter........ 96

Hints When Working With Hiring
Managers/Recruiters.. 97
Your Resume... 99
Sample Resumes... 100
   Single Page Career Summary Resume........ 102
   Functional Resume.. 104
Do's for Your Resume.. 108
Don'ts for Resumes 108
Sample Cover Letter 109
Do's for Cover Letters...111
Don'ts for Cover Letters 111
Networking 112
Prioritize Contacts in New Network 114
How to Start Networking 119
Understanding the Recruitment Process 123
What You Can Say During an Interview.........125
The Art of Negotiation...................................... 130
Keys to Success on Your Journey.....................134

Conclusion 140
References 147
Image References 153

Your Unlimited Opportunities & the Art of Personal Transformation

Introduction 159
Chapter 1: Why Improving Yourself Matters 163
   How Your Past Shapes Your Life 165
   Letting Go 168
   Change the Way You See Yourself 172
Chapter 2: Emotions - The Neuroscience of Emotions 176
   Illness and the Body 178
   Mastering Your Emotions 183
Chapter 3: Taking Action 189
   Focus and Taking the Right Action 191
   How to Take Action 197
Chapter 4: Failure and Risk (Turning Problems Into Opportunities) 202
   Procrastination Cycle 202
   Productive Failure 206
   Inspiration Through Failure 208
   Problem Solving... 211
Chapter 5: Appreciation & Expectation .. 216
   Virtue and Kindness 219
   Gratitude: A Guide... 224
Chapter 6: The Present Moment 229
   Space-Time and Time-Space............................ 231
   Unbiased Thought 236
Chapter 7: Actionable Steps to Change Your Mind 242
   Guide to Meditation... 242
   Walking Meditation... 245

Breath Meditation 248
Heart Coherence.. 252
Chapter 8: Tips to Become the Most Efficient Person Who Can Handle Anything 256
Principles of Self-Learning............................. 258
Myths of Learning 261
The Learning Success Pyramid 265
Chapter 9: Learning - Practical Guidelines.. 271
Methods to Absorb Information Quickly and Easily.. 274
How to Combine Long-Term and Short-Term Memories 279
Conclusion... 285
References 290

Ikigai, How to Choose your Career Path and Discover Your Strengths

Powerful Career Advice to Explore Your Life Potential and Find a Meaningful Job, Especially After Getting Fired, or when Making a Career Change

Clement Harrison

Introduction

"One can choose to go back toward safety or forward toward growth. Growth must be chosen again and again; fear must be overcome again and again."

~ Abraham Maslow

Would it surprise you to discover that statistically 96% of all university graduates are NOT operating in the field they studied in? This fact is based on *personally* interviewing over 10,000 business executives, university graduates, and other business professionals for senior level positions over a five to 10 year period.

Working with specialized executive and technical positions, I first began to notice these trends in 2003. Alarmed and concerned by how high these statistics were, I began investigating further to discover *why* these numbers were so high. I wanted to know what the reasons behind the numbers were, and the only way to discover this was to get the information directly from the source—in this instance, the candidates themselves. The reasons they gave me were even more disconcerting, and I realized that we would soon be experiencing extreme changes in business on multiple levels. I was determined to track as many of these "crossover" candidates as possible. If you can identify with this, or you want to know why each of these highly intelligent, well-educated individuals did what they did, read on...

This book is one that has been a long time in the making. It's jam-packed with more than three decades' experience working with individuals in the job market. Some desperately unhappy, some desperate to make career changes, some feeling so anxious about their futures that it was literally making them ill.

If you can identify with any of the following statements or questions, you've come to the right place, because all the answers are in the pages that follow.

- Are you currently at a crossroads in your career where you're no longer all that excited about getting up in the morning?
- Have you reached the point where you realize that life satisfaction ranks higher on your list of priorities right now than your paycheck?
- Are you currently looking to make a major change in your career, but you're not sure what that looks like?
- Are you searching for something that's going to set your soul alight, reigniting the passion you've felt before, that's now gone?
- Have you been considering a move for some time now?
- Due to economic pressure, has your company just downsized and you've been made redundant?

This list is one that could go on forever because there will always be something that someone is either searching for or unhappy about. *Surprisingly, it's very seldom about the money.*

Are any of the following thoughts keeping you up at night?

- I'm really not happy with my current job.
- I need to make a move, but what career path should I follow?
- Is it too late for a career change?
- Should I leave a comfortable well-paying job if it doesn't make me happy?
- How do I find the right career for me?
- Is it better to have a job that is more meaningful and make less, or find a less meaningful job that pays more?
- What should I take into consideration when looking for a new job?
- Is it reasonable to try to have a career based on your passion?
- How do I learn enough about myself to find a meaningful job?

What are the top reasons for keeping people from finding a job that they love/find meaningful and purposeful? By the end of this journey, you will be armed with enough information to:

- Know more about yourself and what you really want
- Explore various career options available
- Be inspired by other career change success stories that will motivate you to move
- Nail down specific tips for getting the job you really want
- Finding the motivation to start
- Dealing with failure
- Considerations in choosing a career
- Find satisfaction in your next job

If you think this looks like there's a ton of information to assist you all in one place, you're right. It's more important that you discover as much about yourself as possible to decide what you should be doing with your life, not just to earn money, but to find meaning and satisfaction in your work.

This has been part of my life's work for the greater part of 30 years. I have been working closely with people and helping them discover what they're meant to be doing. It's more than filling executive assignments. People are unique, and just as each of us has different DNA that sets us apart, there's something out there that's exclusively for you. Let's discover your destiny, together shall we?

Chapter 1: Assessing Your Current Situation

"Only as you know yourself can your brain serve you as a sharp and efficient tool. Know your own failings, passions, and prejudices so you can separate them from what you see."

—Bernard Baruch

This chapter will discuss the importance of contemplating and understanding your present work environment, circumstances, and experience. It's important to have a clear picture in your mind of where you are now, so you know where you can be in the future. Like everything in life, you cannot begin to progress towards something else or make a decision to stick it out where you are unless you have all the facts. Facts will empower you with the necessary knowledge and information required to make an educated decision. Too often, individuals operate on a whim and it ends up costing them dearly in the long run. Just as you wouldn't move a piece on a chessboard without considering where all the pieces are and whether it's going to put you a few steps ahead, or it could potentially place you in 'checkmate.' You're aiming to be the winner in this instance!

The sub-sections that follow are filled with investigative questions that you should be asking and answering for yourself. The best way to do this is to get a journal, diary, or legal pad and something to write with. If you're anything like me, you may prefer typing things out and keeping the information handy where you can review it often. Whatever your personal preference, the most important thing is to work through each individual question as carefully as possible. There's no time limit on how long this takes you. Because you're dealing with your life plan and some pretty serious questions, they should not be taken lightly or jumped into quickly.

Set aside some quiet time every day where you can work through these without being disturbed. Depending on the environment that you're in, you will appreciate the peace and tranquility of being left alone with your thoughts. If you're going through these at home, it may be worthwhile to get up earlier than everyone else so you have a few hours of quiet time. If you're fortunate enough to work from home, make it quite clear to your family and friends that you won't be available for a specific period of time, even if this means closing yourself off in your study with a "Do Not Disturb" sign on the door.

Investigative questions do exactly that—they investigate, research, discover, prove, disprove, theorize, summarize, and come to conclusions, often needing proof! This is exactly how you need to be looking at each of these questions. It's your life and your future, after all!

Okay, so you have whatever tools you need to jump into these questions; are you ready to take a deep dive into discovering what is really important to you right now? Along with each of the questions, I have given you some further questions that can act as prompts to come to the conclusion that you need to. Before we get there though, you need to accept full responsibility for being honest with yourself. The reason for examining yourself so closely is because you know the person in the mirror better than anyone else. It's only you that can take accountability and responsibility for the choices and decisions you make. As much as we would like to blame the government, the economy, the weather, our parents, our environment, the job market—and the list goes on ad infinitum—you cannot control any of these things. The only thing you do have control over is yourself.

Does it then make perfect sense that we do the work necessary to get you moving in the direction you need to be moving towards? Quite a lengthy introduction, but I cannot overstate the importance of you doing all of this for YOU!

Some of the questions I hear most often from clients and those I meet are, "When do I know that it's time for me to change what I'm doing?" and "What career is right for me?"

One of the biggest challenges facing individuals today is whether they should remain in their careers or not. Before we even begin this exercise, I would like to suggest an excellent tool to assist in getting an overall 'bird's-eye' view of how things look overall is by drawing up a SWOT Analysis. This is a really simple tool to be using (and you can apply it to most aspects of your career and your life). A SWOT Analysis is put together by dividing a sheet of paper into four sections, or, if you are working from a smaller notebook, you might want to dedicate a single page to each of the headings that make up the acronym SWOT. These are:

- Strengths: what are the best talents you possess, characteristics, virtues
- Weaknesses: areas you know you need to work on, personality traits, short-comings
- Opportunities: things you could be considering, new avenues or doors to be opened
- Threats: what can stand in your way, become an obstacle, hold you back

As we work through each of the questions below, take the time to analyze each one as to how they stack up in each of these four areas. You may come across certain questions that can only be classified under one or two of these headings; that's okay. You're looking for the big picture and a clear map of where you need to be. To do that, your strengths and opportunities need to be crystal clear. However, you also need to know what your weaknesses are, and be wary of threats that could come at you from nowhere. I have given you a very brief description of each of these, so you can better understand how to apply them as we work through these exercises.

Analyzing Your Current Position

When answering each of these questions, consider all four areas, and be brutally honest with yourself. If there's something that rubs you the wrong way or irks you about your current position, write it down.

When you think about your current profession, do you love what you do, like what you do, or merely tolerate what you do?

What are your main reasons for feeling the way you do?

We'll assume the middle of the road for the next few questions.

What do you like about your current profession?

Do you have your own parking space, or maybe the canteen makes great food? Another great benefit may be a corner office with a magnificent view!

While these "perks" are nice to have, are they really adding value to your life, and are they making you feel fulfilled as an individual? Are these unwritten perks worth sticking around being constantly miserable?

If you're at the point of merely tolerating your current position, or you've even moved on to genuine disdain, what are the real reasons for you feeling this way? What I'm trying to get at here is whether the things you're really unhappy about can be resolved, or whether you should be updating your CV. Some reasons to be unhappy might be a two- to three-hour commute to and from the office daily in rush-hour traffic that you cannot quite fathom where the "rush" in rush hour comes from. Sitting bumper-to-bumper drives you insane because you can feel the sands of time slipping from your grasp that could be better spent doing something else!

Maybe you're working in an open-plan office environment with some colleagues from hell, or you have a supervisor that's the epitome of a micromanager. Other reasons could be that you're employed by a narcissist and everything is all about them! (And yes, it's a real personality disorder that negatively impacts a work environment). If you are currently unhappy in your career, chances are your list is a long one and will mainly be negative.

Do you see yourself working in the same environment, and the same position for the next three to five years?

This question should be a great indicator as to whether you should be settling in, or planning your exit strategy. Do you physically see yourself in the same position, in the same office, surrounded by the same people? Or are they already physically, mentally, and emotionally exhausting by the end of each day? Are you currently living for Friday afternoons when you get to escape the humdrum routine for some normality because your job is driving you crazy?

Does your current position provide you with opportunities for growth? Do these make you feel excited about your future, or does it leave you feeling impartial instead?

Similar to the question above, do you see yourself going anywhere within the current organization, or do you feel claustrophobic at the prospects of possibly being stuck in a dead-end-rut? You may be in a position that has a glass ceiling; is it one you've already reached?

Are you bored with your current role? Would opportunities working alongside other portfolios or clients pique your interest more?

Have you pitched this to your manager in an attempt to grow into a new and more challenging position? To answer this question, you need to be asking yourself whether you stand up for yourself, asking for what you want out of your position, or if you shrink into the background, too nervous, shy, or scared to come up with strategies that could redefine your role in the business?

Do you have the kind of relationship with your direct superior that would allow you to be open, honest, and direct enough with them to share your ideas? You may be the individual within your organization that has the perfect temperament to be spearheading a particular project or client that others find challenging. At times we are too afraid to ask for what we want and, as a result, we miss out on potentially golden opportunities.

Do I fear change and that's why I'm holding onto my current position?

It's easy to become complacent and comfortable when you've been in the same position for a while. You get stuck in your comfort zone for a number of reasons:

- You know exactly what you're doing
- You know what's expected of you and you deliver
- You are comfortable in your own little space
- You know what deadlines are in place and you're in a routine
- You're afraid of what's out there and whether you'll be successful.
- As mentioned in the introduction, an exceptionally high number of graduate professionals are not working in the field they graduated in! This is one of the reasons for this. When you consider the age and experience of young seniors making career decisions, how much do they really know?
- Do they fully understand the industry they are planning on spending the next 40+ years in?
- Have they considered the impact their decision will have on them for the rest of their lives? Have they chosen to qualify in one particular field for all the wrong reasons?

- Has your course of studies been influenced by somebody else, other than yourself. What was discovered is that there was probably limited understanding. Did you have any notion as to what the work entailed?

- Peer pressure is another reason for choosing to follow a specific career path. You may have wanted to study with your friends.

- Incorrect information provided by guidance counselors, or thanks to family traditions. Whatever the reasons for choosing this career, it was all wrong.

- Even coming from a long line of doctors or lawyers, can you see how assuming your name should be with John Hopkins, or Harvard doesn't make your reasoning correct.

- Maybe you are passionate about one of these professions because you've been exposed to the industry through family bonds. That's an entirely different story, in which event you should be looking forward to a thriving career that may see you performing breakthrough surgery in a specialized field, or being appointed as a judge in your state someday! Note that I used the magic word "*passion.*"

- You've possibly chosen your career because you heard they make a ton of money! There are so many incorrect reasons for making the wrong decision when it comes to your future. Of all of these, money as a motivator is probably the greatest enemy to your success.

So here's my BIGGEST problem with every single one of the above scenarios, and it's probably not what you'd imagine! For each of these individuals who spent anywhere up to seven years qualifying, someone else didn't!

Whether it was in medicine or law or advanced Science, Technology, Engineering, and Math (STEM) qualifications (many of these qualifications are in short supply globally), a spot was taken in an institution that could have trained and upskilled the RIGHT individual. This is not to say that those who have qualified don't make any valuable contributions to their vocations before making the shift (because many of them do). What is sad is that there are usually only limited spaces available at universities, colleges, and other training institutions. It's way more than just taking a slot in their attendance register. It's ALL the other resources that are allocated to the qualification that are skewed and mismanaged. Whether it's training materials to salaries of professors, lecturers, class assistants, tutors—each of these valuable resources are being mismanaged. The most precious commodity of all is one that we can never get back again, no matter what we do—TIME!

Of the thousands of graduate professionals I interviewed and reviewed life and career choices with, many had completed second and third qualifications before they discovered where they "needed to be." All those years were spent learning rather than earning. Were any of them frustrated with themselves? Absolutely! Almost every single one of them wished that they had done things differently.

Are my current skills and talents being utilized sufficiently?

If you are qualified in a specific area and you've been hired to perform duties that are easy, this could lead to frustration. Especially if you feel that your current skills are being wasted. If this is the situation you find yourself in at the moment, you need to either take some initiative and speak with a decision-maker regarding your frustrations, or find out why you are being underutilized. Having this conversation with your superior may not be as comfortable as you would like, but keeping two-way lines of communication between you and management is definitely something you want to foster. Management can only become aware of your feelings if you vocalize them in a civil and productive manner. If you still don't see any improvement within the established time frame, it may be time to reconsider your options. Namely:

- Do you allow them additional time to get the wheels in motion?
- Is it time to start thinking about moving on?
- Are your employers committed to life-long learning and growth for their employees?

Is it part of your employer's company culture to hold regular inhouse and specialized training interventions? Or are you more likely to have access to learning and development opportunities elsewhere? Can you ensure your skills are market-related because you receive the best learning opportunities often? If you are in a more senior position at present, are you providing these opportunities for your own direct reports? Learning doesn't always need to be staid and boring; it can breathe life into an organization to have a light-hearted training session followed by a few team-building exercises. The key objective is that learning should never stop or be shelved. You should always have something on the agenda on at least monthly intervals. Companies that are genuinely interested in ensuring their staff are performing at optimum levels are constantly focused on training such as personal development, emotional intelligence, and industry-aligned specialist training. If you're an accountant, this may mean attending a trade related workshop to be trained in the latest tax directives. Or maybe you're in health and safety, and an update has been passed by the local government. Each of these are necessary for you to perform your duties at your peak, and if your organization cannot see the value in keeping your skills current and on trend, maybe it's time to find a company who will.

Is what you're currently doing in line with your personal value system?

I can totally identify with this line of questioning. Earlier in my career I was doing something completely different. That isn't to say that it was a career that had no value, because it did. The deciding factor for me was losing a close family member. You can probably relate how you go through all the questions about the meaning of life, once again identifying that life is indeed extremely precious and we have no concept of when our time is up. Aside from all of these thoughts, however, another thought crossed my mind and stuck! The question that kept rolling around in my head was, "Will what I'm doing now make a difference in the life of anyone before I die?" It was pretty profound at the time, which is probably why it kept playing over and over in my head for what seemed like an eternity.

One of the reasons it seemed to last forever was that I knew the answer, but was having a hard time coming to terms with it. It was one of those scenarios where you think about what they will say about you at your funeral and how you're likely to be remembered. Stephen Covey in his bestselling book, *The 7 Habits of Highly Effective People* covers an exercise where he gets you to sit down and write your own eulogy (Covey, 1990/2013). I wasn't quite at this point just yet, but it had me questioning the value of my career. I knew immediately that I needed to change, and I needed to get involved with something that was going to make me excited about life and, more importantly, make a difference in the lives of others. It was time for me to make a change!

Signs That You May Need a Change:

Are you constantly feeling physically, mentally, and emotionally exhausted just thinking about work, without even being at work yet? Before answering this question, I'm not referring to being tired after normal physical labor if you've been working on a specific project and it's keeping you on your toes most of the day. This is a feeling where you're permanently drained irrespective of how much sleep you get. You can return home after a day in the office where you've hardly done anything, yet your brain literally hurts. Being drained and tired all the time is not a normal state for the body to be in. Kathy Caprino suggests that the first place you look if you're feeling this way is at your present job! The reason why work can be a major contributor to the way you're feeling is because we spend most of our time there. If you take your commute time, your precious moments with your family, and the time spent sleeping out of your day, you're left with the major chunk of your waking hours spent working. If you hate your job, your boss, or your office environment, the tasks you have to perform become extremely challenging. You may be finding that climbing the corporate ladder is taking longer than you thought. All of these issues make for a toxic work environment that can make you physically ill. If you can identify with any of these, it's time to seriously consider moving on (Caprino, 2012a).

You've become a master at taking the boredom out of your work

Not such an easy challenge to overcome, especially when you've mastered all those things you really don't enjoy doing. This is where you need to begin questioning what your motivation is for staying. Are you afraid of taking a chance on something that's potentially an unknown at this stage? Or do you just prefer the monotony of a job that's safe, secure, and predictable? And yes, there are still (a few) individuals who stick it out with almost one employer their entire working life. Granted, many of these individuals rapidly advance through the ranks, making them extremely valuable to their employers, but there is the added benefit that they are extremely loyal and devoted employees.

It may also be because we've either been doing it for so long, or we're too afraid to take a risk when it comes to making a career change, so we stick with it. It has become a habit that we clock into the office every morning and complete the tasks we hate, but we've become so used to it that we hardly even realize our satisfaction level is virtually non-existent.

Are you prepared to sacrifice your sanity for a salary?

Too many people stick it out with jobs they really hate all for the sake of money. Is your salary really that important when you consider how bored you are? Getting used to a great salary makes so many people stick with jobs they hate for years. They seldom have opportunities for growth or promotion, but receive decent bonuses and annual increases, making that carrot look very appealing, while the current level of boredom in their work leaves them feeling hollow inside.

A quick sidebar on the carrot and the stick—you do realize that the donkey never gets the carrot, EVER, right?

Another key observation by Caprino is that there will come a time when even the biggest salary pales in comparison with finding meaningful work that's going to add to your self-worth as an individual. Once you reach this point in your career you start putting yourself first, ahead of an organization. Whether we realize it or not, we often form the cogs in the wheels that turn industry, but job satisfaction should be right up there almost at the top of our list of priorities. As mentioned briefly in the introduction, the REAL reason most individuals leave their jobs seldom has anything to do with money!

Making all the "right" choices doesn't guarantee job satisfaction. Why not?

This is getting to the heart of the reason most individuals eventually give up studying in one field and move in another direction. For them, they managed to identify the problem early enough (while still studying), rather than once in the workplace. To put it as simply as possible, they made the choice that was right for someone else! It wasn't necessarily their decision to study in the field that they're now bored to death with. The decision was made to please a parent, peers, student advisors, whoever. They were actually the last person on the list who had any say, and it's now finally become crystal clear that they're stuck in a rut.

Do you ever feel that your life could be better spent doing something else?

This was the point I got to when I finally had to ask the tough question—"Is what I'm doing today going to make a difference in anyone's life?" For others, the questions may be that there has to be more to life than what they're currently doing and experiencing. So what then is actually holding you back? As you assess and analyze each of these questions, you need to begin asking yourself those questions that are tough to answer. It's your life and believe me, you were made to do great things—you just need to believe in your own talents and abilities, rather than trying to live someone else's dream for them (Caprino, 2013).

Speaking with life coach Karen Elizaga and author of *Find Your Sweet Spot*, there are a couple of ways you can discover for yourself if your time has come to change careers. A couple of points she makes can be useful to consider before throwing in the towel. Her story is an interesting one. She also studied law, ended up working her way up in a legal firm, doing things she hated day in and day out. While she loved working with people, she hated the argumentative and contentious nature of her work. It took her 13 years to tough it out and finally make the decision to move (Elizaga, 2014).

How did she come to the final realization that practicing law was not her passion? By putting into practice what I've already given you at the beginning of the chapter. Karen wrote out her strengths and weaknesses, and added another list to the equation—who in the immediate surroundings may be able to make use of what you can offer? This is probably going to require some "out of the box" thinking. It's now pulling yourself completely out of the environment you're in and making you consider other industries that may be able to utilize your specific strengths towards something else. This could open new doors and opportunities to you, just like Elizaga was able to bring her passion for people together to coach them especially in changing careers.

Another recommendation is to consider what you like and don't like in a working environment. Very few individuals stop and consider WHY they want to move in the first place. If you can't pinpoint exactly what it is that's making you unhappy (your dislike(s)) you could move onto the next environment and simply get more of the same. All that's going to achieve is jumping from the frying pan directly into the fire.

She refers to another two important questions to answer relating to your current work experience:

What are your performance reviews telling you?

While you may think it's a great idea to move on, consider what your current performance reviews have to say about what you're doing. If you are good at your job, the chances of your review indicating this are highly probable. The time to start worrying about whether you've found your niche or not is when your performance reviews indicate a need for improvement, or overall poor work performance. (You won't deliver your best work if you're not enjoying your job.)

Job satisfaction and your paycheck

We've mentioned the amount of money regarding salary expectations above, but are you so passionate about what you are doing that you'd be prepared to do it for nothing? There's a famous quotation by Confucius that says, "Choose a job you love, and you will never have to work a day in your life." The lesson to be learnt from this quotation is that whatever you do in life should be something that you love to do! If you're merely staying in your current job for the paycheck, chances are you're beginning to feel discouraged and frustrated with your work.

Some other excellent advice comes to reminiscing and reflecting on your current career. Too often we dwell on the past (which keeps us there and prevents us from moving forward). If you've been in the wrong career and you know you have to change, don't waste valuable time and precious energy beating yourself up about time wasted in another position, field, or industry. The truth is that no matter where you are in your career today, how long you studied, and how many years you've been doing what you've been doing, don't label this as a waste of precious time as many do. Experience in any industry is valuable and you can carry this over to your next position. There's no such thing as wasted learning. Knowledge is power, and as far as experience goes, many will pay handsomely to have the expertise that you may possess.

When moving on isn't always the right thing

Defining your strengths, weaknesses, likes, and dislikes is a vital part of this exercise to decide whether the time is right for you to be thinking about moving on or taking that leap of faith. Moving is not always what's best in every situation. When you attend an interview to change positions, you cannot always tell exactly what the environment will be like once you get there. As a matter of fact, it's usually completely different once you settle in. This difference could prove to be worse than where you were previously.

An example of this might include the team that you join. You may never meet them officially before accepting the company's offer and they may leave you totally underwhelmed! The work itself may have sounded challenging and exciting during the interview, but once you settle in, it may be way more boring than where you've just come from. Another consideration should be that you are once again beginning at the bottom of the food chain in a new environment. Progression within the organization may be more limited, or slower than you were led to believe in your interview. Remember that if an organization wants to hire you, they are going to present the company in the best possible light, and promising you the world could be one way to secure your buy-in! (Evans, 2014).

Chapter 2:
Finding Your Way

"The best day of your life is the one on which you decide your life is your own. No apologies or excuses. No one to rely on or blame. The gift is yours, it's an amazing journey and you alone are responsible for the quality of it."

~ Bob Moawad

In this chapter, we will discuss how you can figure out what you should be doing with your career. Sometimes it is easier to know what you don't want for you to discover what you do want.

Are You Stuck or In Limbo?

One of the worst feelings in the world is having to drag yourself into work each day, knowing that you don't want to be there. This is only made worse when you're feeling stuck and you don't know where you belong in the world. You're uncertain of your career choices and where you want to be. It's having the feeling that you're prepared to be "anywhere but here!" The only way to move beyond this point is by identifying exactly what's causing you to feel 'stuck' where you are now. This could be due to several reasons such as being afraid or unsure of the unknown and what the future holds. Let's face it, change is scary for the most part, but even more so when you aren't sure whether you're making the right decision.

Many times, the frustration we feel in our careers comes from living out someone else's dream career rather than your own. The amazing thing about life is that you can achieve anything you want to achieve by making the right career choices. Decisions that are aligned with your core beliefs and your value system. You can never be truly happy unless you're living out your own purpose, rather than one that belongs to someone else. Figuring out your purpose is what will drive you towards the career that will resonate within you and feel like 'home.'

Discovering WHY?

Discovering and identifying your 'why' will help you move out of an environment where you're feeling stuck, or you no longer belong. How do you get to your 'why'? Once again, this takes a lot of quiet introspection, getting thoughts, feelings, and emotions onto paper. It's once again being able to ask difficult questions to figure out why you are feeling stuck in your current rut. One of the best ways of doing this is by writing out a purpose statement that puts into words why you are working in your current position and why you've chosen the lifestyle you have. This will make you consider your current value system and what's important to you at this present moment.

As we grow and mature, gain new experiences, and are exposed to new ideas, our motivations for doing things change. What was important to us five or even 10 years ago versus what's important now could be completely different. Your group of friends may have changed; you may be ready to settle down. Here are a few pointers on how to discover your 'why,' what it is, and the impact it can have on your career.

Your 'why' should not make you feel anxious, overwhelmed, or unfulfilled. Instead, it should be an important part of figuring out where you need to be on your career path.

Discovering the 'why' behind what you're meant to be doing, versus what you're currently doing is probably one of the scariest things to deal with. It's recognizing that you're uncomfortable in your current position while being able to put your finger on what you would like to be doing with solid reasons to back this up. Remember I mentioned towards the end of chapter 1 that money is seldom the only motivator to move, and also moving may not be the best of ideas? If you can discover the 'why' with all its sub-categories, and clearly identify each of these, it will give you a clearer image of the route you need to follow.

Stephen Warley describes not understanding your 'why' as being in "limbo or stuck in purgatory." You remain in a fixed "holding pattern" while the rest of the world continues to progress and move forward. The following is a list of recommendations he makes to clearly define your 'why':

Your 'why' will lead you towards the actions you need to take in your career.

- It can help you identify what your calling is in life.

- Once you've discovered your 'why,' your resolve and conviction to move forward will be strengthened.

- It becomes your driving motivation to succeed in your career; the thing that moves you forward.

- Your 'why' will help define you as an individual, bringing out personality traits and qualities necessary to succeed.

- Your levels of productivity will be increased because you're doing what you love.

- Your 'why' forms the background and basis for your "mission statement" for your career and your life.

- It becomes the reality of your life's work and weaves a golden thread through your career history, if not your life.

- Discovering your 'why' will influence when, where, and how your decisions are made. Many of these decisions will influence your future.

- Your 'why' will lead you to a clearer vision of your life's work.

Changing Careers

A decision to change careers won't always be supported by everyone, and there may be times where you will stand against the rest of the world. You may not be successful immediately. It may take time in the beginning, and as most successful individuals know, nothing comes easily. It will always require both sacrifice and hard work. You may not see results for an extended period of time. Those who make it are usually the ones who are prepared to see it through; they're prepared to fail if necessary and accept responsibility for their own actions.

When changing direction and careers, you may have obstacles that you need to overcome. These won't always be easy but are usually necessary in achieving success.

Discovering your 'why' begins with knowing and understanding who you are. You get to this point through the emotional intelligence step of self-awareness. If you think you've got a complete grip on who you are and what you're all about, there's a whole lot more to it than just that. It's understanding your emotions and your feelings, being sensitive to what they are telling you at any given time. Self-awareness helps you communicate with others by engaging with them on a level that works for both of you.

If I had to ask you what the real reason is for sticking it out in your current position, what are you likely to say, if you were to be 100% honest? Which of the following answers would best describe why you're holding onto your job?

- It's a job and I need the money.
- I'm currently drowning in debt and I can't risk being without a salary.
- All my friends are working in this industry.
- My spouse wants me to work for this company for the benefits.
- It's what my parents suggested I do.
- It's a job I thought was financially sustainable and with high earning potential.

How do you discover your 'why'?

Analyze Yourself

The recommendations continue to correlate with self-analysis that we began in chapter one. This means some more thinking and more writing. This time I want you to write randomly every day about your day and the things you've enjoyed or noticed. Maybe it's situations that have taken place at work. Set aside 15-30 minutes each day to include this information in a journal where you can refer back to it whenever necessary.

In the same journal, make some notes about your feelings towards each of the following:

- Principles: what makes up your moral code? Where do you draw the line on things that you're prepared to do or not?

- What drives you towards achieving your goals? This could also be identified by what motivates you.

- Again we need to analyze what you're truly passionate about? What would you be prepared to do for nothing?

- Re-analyze your strengths from chapter 1. Are there any additional strengths that you may want to add to your original list? These may be strengths you're currently using.

- What would your perfect workday look like? What would you be doing? Who would you be meeting with, or associating with? (This answer is especially powerful).

- It's important that you keep accurate records of your thoughts, your moods, and your actions for a period of time so you can possibly see a pattern forming.

Analyze Your Role

Place your current role under a microscope and analyze it. Go through your career step by step. What attracted you to your current position in the first place? What have you managed to accomplish over your career so far? Have there been highlights that you're particularly proud of? Have you ever been recognized for your accomplishments? What were these, and how did the recognition make you feel? When are you most productive? When do you feel most drained? What part of your work are you most passionate about? This will be what you can probably do with ease and it makes you feel most complete. For each of these questions, go back over your answers, and ask yourself WHY for each of them. Try to be as honest, and thorough as possible.

Think about who inspires you to achieve. Maybe it's not a person but rather the recognition or reward that motivates you to do what you do. If there are things that frustrate you or make you feel angry, take note of what these are. If it's something you will never be able to change, then you need to either learn to accept that as a fact or decide about moving onto something better.

Are there certain things that you've thought about doing ever since you were a child, or things you enjoy doing in your spare time? Two questions are attached to this thought process. The first is, do you continue with these activities in your spare time? Secondly, if you never had to worry about money, would you still be doing what you're currently doing?

When identifying skills and strengths, what kinds of things do people always ask for your assistance with?

What product or service would you sell and what job you could do, other than what you're doing now?

What does the world really need that you are able to offer? Will it help to solve a specific problem or meet the demands of an industry or marketplace? If so, is this a long-term demand? Will this still be around in the next 10 years or so?

Another great idea is to ask those closest to you for their input. Allow them to comment as to what they believe your strengths to be and what industry they believe you should be working in; however, be sure to ask them for reasons why!

The final few steps in discovering your 'why' is to answer these five questions:

- Are you looking for job satisfaction or ultimate fulfilment in your work?
- What are you able to do daily that is effortless, yet pushes you to develop as a person and learn more about your job and who you are?
- What excites you most about your current position?
- What provides you with the greatest challenges, but motivates you in the workplace?
- What would your ultimate job look like?

Discovering Your Ikigai

The word Ikigai comes from a combination of two Japanese words: iki, which means 'life,' and kai, described as "your reason for being." Kai can also be interpreted as your reason for wanting to get up in the morning. According to People at Heart, it combines hopefulness along with doing the things you love to do (People at Heart Coaching, n.d.).

Your Ikigai is completely unique to you and you alone. It provides you with a sense of purpose and may often point you in the direction you need to go to feel fulfilled. It is not subjected to who you are, what position you hold, how much money you have in the bank, or any of the other conventional career testing strategies. The Ikigai comes from Okinawa in Japan and appears to date back to the Heian period in Japanese history (794 to 1185). This is according to Akihiro Hasegawa, who completed a white paper on the subject in 2001. There are also numerous words to describe this, but they all pretty much come down to describing your life's work, once you find those points that overlap on a Venn diagram (Mitsuhashi, 2017).

A study conducted in 2010 by the Central Research Services investigated approximately 2,000 Japanese men and women regarding their life value according to Ikigai. Only 31% of these surveyed identified work as their Ikigai. For this reason, it's seldom money that's the main motivating factor. While work may be a factor, it's very seldom the only factor (Suzuki & Central Research Services Inc, n.d.). According to Yukari Mitsuhashi, "ikigai is the main reason for getting up in the morning" (Mitsuhashi, 2017).

The well-known psychologist Mieko Kamiya states that "Japanese people believe that the sum of small joys in everyday life results in more fulfilling life as a whole" (Kamiya, 1966). The people of Japan boast some of the world's longest-living population. Women's average age is 87 years old, while their male counterparts live to be about 81 years old. This is according to statistics by the Department of Health, Labor, and Welfare.

Your Ikigai brings you joy by doing those things that are meaningful in your life. It helps create a sense of purpose, rather than living life on other people's terms. Your skills are being used for something worthwhile, and you are making a difference in the lives of those you come into contact with.

How do you begin identifying your Ikigai?

There are two ways one can go about this. Begin with a Venn diagram with four overlapping circles. In each of the different circles, write down the following:

- I'm especially good at…?
- Things I love doing…?
- What can I be paid for doing…?
- What does the world need most…?

The second option is to write out three separate lists:

- Things you're good at doing
- What would you like to be doing
- Your value system

Where these three lists intersect is recognized as your Ikigai, although it's only once you can actually put these things into action that they then become your Ikigai (Buettner, 2008).

Further Career Considerations

So you've made all these notes and asked yourself all these important questions regarding your next career. Have you considered all of your options, though? You've identified your passion and where you think you'd like to go with your next career, but are you ready to take the major plunge?

Kathy Caprino warns of mistakes that can easily be made, but are easily avoided if you're aware of them beforehand. These mistakes include looking at the world through rose-tinted glasses. Where we aren't realistic in our expectations from the future, the best way to indicate what the future will hold is by looking at the past. Consider what you've already achieved in your career so far. What has gone right, and what has gone wrong? There's a reason for being realistic when answering these questions—you need to be honest, accountable, and realistic about what the future holds. She mentions five common mistakes made by most individuals wishing to change careers.

Leaving Change Too Late

Kathy shares her own story as an example of this mistake. She waited until things were so bad within her previous position that she literally ran screaming from the position she was so desperately unhappy in. All she was interested in was getting as far away from where she was as possible, and she ended up in another position that wasn't right for her. What normally happens in this scenario is that it takes you a lot longer to find where you do belong, because you try to escape anything and everything that even remotely represents where you were. This is not always a good thing because you end up wasting valuable time, effort, and energy doing something else that's not right for you. In Kathy's case, she needed to spend a few more years doing something else before she found her ideal position. She recommends that if there are areas of your career that you need to improve on, do this before moving onto a new career. It's way easier to firm up on new skills and talents when you have the safety net of a current position where you're earning and have the stability of an income, rather than attempting to develop these skills on your own while trying to build a new business or reputation. If you have relationships that need to be mended, do so in order that wherever you go you don't have the possibility of repairing relationships once you've gone.

She shares four ingredients that are vital when considering your move:

Clarity: Know exactly what it is that you want to be doing, almost to the point that you can feel it and taste it.

Commitment: This is not the time to be see-sawing between moves, trying to decide whether you should make the change or not. Once you've made the commitment (like any other commitment), see it through. If you're not 100% behind your decision to move, then maybe you shouldn't be thinking about moving just yet. Consider that there may be things unresolved in your current position that need to be finalized first.

Confidence: Having confidence in your new career is what will get you by and also allow others to not only respect you, but to take you seriously. If you're a shrinking violet, or act sheepishly because you're uncertain of yourself, it's definitely time to reconsider your strategy and whether you have made the right decision.

Courage: It takes guts and determination to leave a position that you've had for a fairly long time. Walking away from everything that you know and that feels comfortable to you is never something that's easy to do. It is important, however, especially when changing careers entirely. Without courage to try something new, you're essentially dead in the water.

Additional skills necessary are linked to your emotional well-being, your financial well-being or stability, and having a professional attitude.

One of the most important of these is having sufficient finances in place to support you, especially if you're moving out on your own. This takes way more than you would imagine initially. You should have enough money set aside to support you for a six-month period if the economy is in a normal condition, and even more so during economic downturns or financial slumps. This is one of the main reasons why new business models fail. They have insufficient funds available to support them as well as other operational business costs over this period.

Understanding that you don't only need enough capital for a salary during this period, but you need to calculate all other business operating expenses. If you cannot raise sufficient funding for a loan or have enough money set aside for between six and nine months, then cut back on your expenses, put more money away into a savings fund, or look for alternate funding (such as a business partner) that can assist with this. There are plenty of other options available for business funding. Investigate each of these until you find the model that works best for you.

Be Clear On What You Want

Before jumping ship, it's important that you identify exactly what you'd like to be doing. This is the reason for writing down those things that you like doing, versus those things you don't enjoy. Every single position will have aspects that you won't enjoy. Figure out what you thrive on doing and what it takes to do this. What industries do you enjoy working in? Do you enjoy communicating with individuals over the phone, or thrive on physical face-to-face interactions instead? Are you better working in an office, or do you need to be outside in nature to really feel alive? Do you live for putting boardroom presentations together and delivering these to executives regularly, or are you more suited to a back-office support position where you're out of the public eye? Do you prefer working with numbers than people?

All these questions need to be asked and answered so you can get a much better understanding of what you really want and not what you think you want out of your next position. Are there specific people that always seem to rub you the wrong way? (And there always will be these—it is humanly impossible for everyone to be able to get along with every other individual). It's the reason why we are all individuals and humans to begin with. Decide what the next company needs to look like in terms of their values and possibly even their mission statement. What ideals would you like to see within the organization's corporate culture? This often speaks to ethics, integrity, loyalty, how they deal with customers. Are they honest in their business dealings?

What type of management team are you hoping to work with or report to? Do you know how you like to be managed? Some individuals prefer to be managed closely with a micro-management relationship; others choose for that type of management to be at the bottom of the list. A number of years ago, I had an employee who would stand in the doorway of my office several times a day and the words that came out of her mouth were always, "I'm so sorry to bother you, this may be a stupid question, but..." Now, let me say that my management style is actually situational! It depends on what each staff member needs, or what the circumstances require at the time. One of the styles of management I least enjoy is micro-management, possibly because I never enjoyed being micro-managed myself. My response to this staff member would always be, "There's no such thing as a stupid question." I was and still am a firm believer that I would rather have someone ask me something if they are uncertain, rather than trying to close the barn door once the horse has bolted, so to speak!

You need to identify what you are prepared to settle for and what's non-negotiable for you; this will save you a lot of disappointment further down the line in your career.

Let's Talk Money...

I've mentioned that reasons for leaving a position are seldom about money, and for the most part this is true, although you need to be realistic and already have a number in your mind as to what you're worth. If you're not certain about this, do some research online about what someone with your qualifications and experience in your industry is worth. Have a number in mind before you walk into an interview for your next position. Take what you're currently getting into consideration. If you have a pension plan, the next position should also at least have a 401K. Medical benefits, travel or car allowances, bonuses, commission checks—everything needs to be accounted for. Consider what you're prepared to negotiate on and what's completely non-negotiable for you. It's important that you have all these numbers memorized or written down somewhere before you negotiate a deal with anyone. The last thing you need is to walk out of a negotiation worse off than you are now.

Finding My Strengths

If you find it difficult to identify your strengths and interests on your own, there are many assessments available online that can help you determine specific natural abilities necessary to do well in certain industries. Many years ago, aptitude tests formed part of a basic education curriculum to help students identify careers that were best suited to them. This was not always a guaranteed assessment; however, it provided a number of options for someone to choose from.

Most large corporations make use of an assessment tool to provide them with a slightly better understanding as to the suitability of the candidate to their requirements. Both inhouse and external recruiters may also choose to use these assessments to try to eliminate an incorrect hiring decision. Unfortunately, some of these assessments are flawed and can be manipulated depending on what's happening with the candidate at the time of taking the assessment. The more the assessment is based on 'behavioral' attributes, the higher the possibility of manipulation. To give you an idea of how easily this can happen:

Situation One:

The candidate is due for an interview with an organization and oversleeps. Racing to try to make up for the lost time, they almost fall down the stairs, tripping over the family dog. Murphy's law would have them stuck in traffic, getting caught at each red light on their way to your office. They manage to race in, flustered but just in time for the interview. From the moment they arrive, they are handed a pile of forms to fill in that goes into such detail that one of the few things it doesn't require is their mother's maiden name! Completing a behavioral analysis under stress, they would answer the various questions completely differently to the following situation.

Situation Two:

The candidate wakes up the moment their alarm goes off. Their clothing is already set aside waiting for them. They have time for a healthy breakfast and can leave early enough to avoid any traffic that may cause a delay. They arrive at the interview ten to fifteen minutes early and can take their time completing all the necessary documentation.

The way that these two candidates would respond to 'behavioral' based assessments will be completely different, given the two circumstances. This would apply to any assessment that requires an emotive, behavioral response.

Recruitment used to base their hiring decision on intellectual quotient (IQ), which is the ability to work with scientific equations, problems and come up with creative solutions. This is no longer the case, thanks to the way the world of work has changed. These skill requirements have now evolved to those emotional intelligence (EQ) instead. This determines how well you are able to work with others and regulate your own emotions.

As you search the internet to prepare yourself for these assessments, or to find those positions best suited to your skills, look for assessments in each of the following areas. For each of these assessments, links are provided in the Resource section below.

Emotional intelligence: Free Emotional Intelligence Tests via, My Personality, Global Leadership, Greater Good, Positive Psychology

Career Aptitude: 123 Career Test, CareerExplorer, Skills Profiler

Personality Tests: Myers-Briggs, Keirsey Temperament Sorter, Enneagram, 16personalities

Interests: MyNextMove, iSeek, MAPP Test, CareerOneStop, Interest Assessment

There are many assessments available that can point you in the right direction. The more assessments you can identify with, the more likely you are to be searching for the right match when it comes to a career.

Chapter 3:
Exploring Alternative Careers

"The most difficult thing is the decision to act, the rest is merely tenacity. The fears are paper tigers. You can do anything you decide to do. You can act to change and control your life, and the procedure, the process is its own reward."

~ Amelia Earhart

In this chapter, we're going to look at exploring various job options so you become aware of possible career choices. You may not realize it at the moment but there are so many more opportunities than you could ever imagine, if you are prepared to look beyond your current industry, position, and even your present career.

Online Assessments

By now, you've been able to complete various career tests and assessments online that may have given you some further insight into various careers. It's important to look at these assessments holistically, rather than independently from one another. The more similar crossovers through multiple tests and assessments, the greater the likelihood that some of these careers or jobs may be the right fit for you. Coming to an answer and choosing the best possible career for you shouldn't be the first name that appears on a list or search engine! One way to achieve this is by making lists of the career recommended following your assessments.

These tests will usually present you with a variety of career choices that are suited to your personality type and various strengths. This can be a good starting point. Once you have extensive lists of potential career choices in front of you, begin going through each item on the list independently. If you clearly understand all of the dimensions of the career listed (the good, the bad, and the ugly), and you know that this work is not suited to your skills, or your interest, scratch it off your list. The moment you come to a career that you don't know, it's time to begin researching as much as you can on what this career entails. Not knowing what an 'actuary' does, doesn't mean that it's not the correct route for you to take. If you already know what you should be doing, make certain that it's listed as one of the career options against your assessments. As frustrating as this sounds, this may well be one of those careers that you've been advised to pursue by school mates, parents, teachers, or other family members. You may be so brainwashed with the idea that this is what you have to do, that you've shut yourself off from anything and everything else.

Be Realistic in Your Expectations

Go into this process with an open mind, believing that anything is possible, rather than limiting yourself with only a handful of options. The annual *Occupational Outlook Handbook* is an excellent source of career information for you to consider doing research through. It has some interesting information regarding those who have just graduated from a university or college. Be realistic and look for the entry-level career that's right for you. I would often need to educate and re-educate new graduates regarding their career expectations. Many would apply for top-paying jobs, or those that required years of experience, only to feel let down by the system when they were turned away. Qualifying as a 'lawyer,' for instance, doesn't automatically give you the necessary courtroom experience to be responding for a position that is going to fast-track you to the role of a senate judge. It takes years to reach this level of expertise, and you need to develop more than just a track record. If you've just completed your studies, look for entry level positions first. These will be best suited because they often come with mentors and others who are able to guide you. These same positions normally have strategies in place to fast-track careers already built in. The fact that it's an entry-level job doesn't always mean that it's right at the bottom of the food chain and you're going to be given all of the grunt work. However, it's still recommended you make certain of this. You don't want to have to start off in the mailroom all over again when you're already experienced in middle management.

Investigating the Unknown

When investigating positions or industries that you don't know, there are a couple of other ways you can go about it. Firstly, you can speak with others who are in the same industry or working in the same positions. Ask them specific questions that you'd like answers to, trying to ask open-ended questions. Some ideas for questions are listed below:

- What does your typical day look like from start to finish?
- What are some of the challenges you've had to overcome in your position?
- When have you found your position to be most rewarding?
- Is there room to grow?
- What is the typical route one would follow when being promoted, or advancing in your career?
- How quickly are you able to be promoted? Is this dependent on the industry you're working in, or company specific?
- What do you most enjoy about the work you do?
- What do you dislike in your current position?

If you are speaking with someone who knows you, be candid and straightforward with them—ask them if this is the right job for you.

Wherever possible, speak to more than one person so that you're not getting a biased opinion. You are trying to obtain sufficient information for you to decide that's going to affect you for quite a while, especially if you don't intend job-hopping for the first couple of years of your working career.

Network or Attend Conferences

Another way for you to obtain as much information as possible is by attending networking events that are specific to the industry you're considering. In doing so, don't be afraid to introduce yourself to people and ask loads of questions. They will be able to relate to where you are now. Remember that everyone needed to start off somewhere. It's an added advantage to become as informed as possible, rather than regretting your decision and being stuck where you shouldn't be.

Additional sources of information are available through online videos and tutorials. In these videos, they will even provide you with the specific educational qualification necessary that will provide you with access to the career. However, having the piece of paper that qualifies you to work in an industry is not a guarantee that you will find work in that market.

Look at Pay Scales

Here's some of the information you need to gather for yourself so you can make an 'informed' decision that this is the right career for you.

Check Glassdoor, PayScale or any other local salary scale websites for salary levels. It's important that you look at the bottom end of the averages and ask yourself whether you'd be able to survive on that if you managed to secure one of these jobs. Remember to subtract any statutory deductions that you may be liable for, so that you come out to the correct net amount that you would walk away with, and not the amount before tax.

Assess the job description, comparing it to your current or previous ones, and see what it has that your other jobs didn't. If the requirements are almost identical to what you were doing previously, consider whether your move will be the wisest decision or whether you're likely to encounter the same issues you had in your previous jobs.

Career Prospects or Not?

Check the long-term opportunities associated with this career. It might just be a job for experience, but not for the long term. Of all the information you've been gathering up to this point, this is one of the most important pieces of data to gather. For any industry, a career is going to be in one of three places:

On the Rise: This means that this industry is growing and work will likely be around for many years to come. Studying in this field and obtaining a qualification is a safe bet, and you are likely to find employment. An example of this type of job would be in the field of artificial intelligence or robotics, any of the fields in advanced science, technology, electronics, math, or even computer coding. Each of these fields are currently in demand. The question is, will they still be in demand five to 10 years from now?

Stable: Industries that are stable are those that aren't likely to go out of fashion. These are careers that will always be in demand because every industry has a need for them. Examples of these careers include human resources, law, medicine, sales, marketing, information technology, teaching, nursing, and a variety of other positions.

In Decline: There are a number of careers that are in decline at the moment. These are careers that have reached a saturation point. There are too many individuals who are qualified in these industries.

The Information Technology Age: A Case Study

An example of this could be basic computer programming that was initially introduced at the same time that computers were first introduced into the market in the 1980s. Everyone wanted to be part of the latest trend to hit the marketplace. With the mass interest in all things computer and information technology, other careers began to suffer. Within the information technology realm at the moment, unless you are extremely good at what you are doing or shifting your focus to artificial intelligence (AI), robotics, or coding, the market is fairly saturated.

Those who got involved within the IT market in the 80s still have a good few years to operate within the current market and chances are, if they've kept abreast of changes or decided to specialize, their skills are still in high demand. These are all considerations you need to be aware of. Unless you are moving into a specific niche within an industry that is showing growth or has the prospect of growing, my recommendation would be to err on the side of caution rather than jumping in with both feet. If you find that this is one of the industries or markets that you plan on studying within, please reconsider your choice and look for something that you will still be passionate about but will sustain you for years to come.

> *<u>Sidebar</u>: An interesting thing happened when everyone jumped onto the IT bandwagon in the 80s. Other industries that would have shared in many of these students had fewer enrolments. This trend would not be felt for a number of decades, although it was there.*
>
> *The marketplace's current skills shortage is just one example of this trend. These are all items you need to take into consideration when choosing to study, or a career that you plan on spending most of your life working within.*

So much of this chapter has been dedicated to those starting out in their first careers or planning on what to study in college or university that's going to provide them with sufficient money and job satisfaction. But what about those like Kathy Caprino, who allowed things to get so bad that she literally packed up her desk and ran as fast and as far away as she could? Before making such a rash decision, here are a couple of sobering pointers for you to consider very carefully and realistically.

Can I Afford to Step Back into an Entry Level Position?

This is essentially what you would be doing if you are going to change careers mid-stream. This is one of the reasons we got you to assess and research with PayScale or Glassdoor. If you have sufficient savings tucked away to support you with the difference for as long as you believe it's going to take you to claw your way back up the corporate ladder, then by all means, you have a safety net to fall back on. Alternately, your spouse is earning a great salary and you can afford to take the salary sacrifice for a while.

Do I Need Any New Skills?

While it's great to consider moving onto a new position and now chasing after your dream job, one of the questions to ask yourself is whether you have all the right skills necessary to do the job or if you need to learn new things to make yourself more marketable. If you need specific skills, how can you achieve these without jeopardizing your current position? You see, my recommendation would be for you to do all of this upfront studying and gathering new skills and abilities from the very comforts of your current job (after hours of course). With so many online portals and training available, you are able to gain additional certification or credits towards the career of your choice within weeks or months. It's better to do this and enter the field with qualifications that are relevant to the industry, even if you have years' worth of work experience in another industry or industries. If you've identified skills you don't have as of yet, look at how you can obtain these through online courses or enrolling with online training facilities. Some of these institutions offer free online training in a multitude of disciplines.

Do Your Research

Do your own homework to find out what skills are in demand. You can begin on job portals, cross-referencing current positions that are offering the right pay scale you're accustomed to. If you have a specific preference as to the company or industry you'd like to be working in, you could always begin with their internal openings first. This will require more than looking at job titles (these can often be deceiving). What one company refers to as a specific job title may be equal to something completely different within another department or company. Compare job requirements across each of these positions, rather than the designation given by the hiring officer or recruitment professional. See which of these best match your career skills. If there are skills that you don't have yet that appear in most of the positions you'd like to move into, these are the skills you need to consider acquiring.

Find A Way to Showcase Your New Skills

Many companies are regularly looking for individuals to sacrifice their time and talents for the sake of a good cause. This may be the ideal opportunity for you to prove yourself of value, without seeking reimbursement or reward. The main thing that you are looking for in this instance is a way to showcase your talent to help solve problems or prove that you know what you're talking about. Some other recommendations according to Alan Henry are to begin your own blog that's directed at the specific industry (to prove that you know what you're talking about) or volunteering your time to help out with companies within this niche (Henry 2013).

This will allow you to become known in the industry, and you could also begin building your network.

Consider Your V.I.P.S.

Leslie Helmuth reported that according to Linda Spencer from Harvard, there are a number of steps you should be considering before you make your final move. The first of these is known as VIPS for short, and stands for some pretty standard characteristics that you should already be considering (Helmuth, 2015):

Values: What values and ideals are non-negotiable in your career, no matter where you go? Unfortunately, this is something you will only really discover once you make the transition. You can do some basic homework by searching for what individuals who work for the organization are likely to say about their experience working there. This is often freely available on job boards and hiring sites such as Indeed.

Interests: You need to keep your work movements aligned with your interests to keep you motivated and moving forward. If you are not motivated to continue moving, it's unlikely that you will stick with any changes if they don't interest you. This is where you can refer back to the online assessments and other tests taken, as well as the list where you've indicated the commonalities of each of these. Mark these down as your interests.

Personality: Your personality is what defines you, and if you're uncertain of what some of these personality traits are, try the Enneagram assessment or the 16 Personalities test. Excellent Emotional Intelligence assessments could also assist you in identifying personality. In most instances, your personality is innate and there's not too much you can do about it unless you are consciously aware of shortcomings that you need to work on. Even knowing that you are facing certain limitations, it may take you a lifetime of conscious effort to make changes that will alter your personality. It's better to know upfront what these limitations are; that way you don't go rushing headlong into a position that is going to challenge each of your personal limitations. It's always better to be able to play towards your strengths instead.

Skills: If you've been working for a given length of time, you have developed skills that are specific to the work that you've done. Chances are you've also developed what we refer to as skills of the future. Some of these include being able to integrate with and work effectively with cross-cultural teams to come up with creative problem-solving techniques. You may have negotiation skills or be able to manage teams effectively. Meeting deadlines might be your thing, or you may be great when it comes to working with the public. Don't sell yourself short when looking to make a move. Each of the skills you have gained over the years has a different value attached to it, and while you may not possess a qualification to move into another career, you may possess all the right skills and abilities.

Put A Plan Together

Before making any moves, put a plan in place that will allow you to see where you have come from (in the past), where you are now (your present position), and naturally where you see yourself going (the future). This means having the ability to be subjective about your past experiences, what they have taught you, what you've been able to carry with you into your present position (possibly honing these skills and talents), and what you could possibly refine even further to get to where you want to be. It's all a question of how many of your talents and skills can be redeveloped and reassigned into something new. Are they skills and talents that you enjoy using (Hulmuth, 2015)?

Another step that you need to take in making your plan functional is by updating your CV and making certain that the appropriate talents, skills, and abilities are highlighted sufficiently. Whatever you do, when putting your CV together to change careers, don't stretch the truth to accommodate any of the job requirements! Recruiters have noses like bloodhounds and they're going to go right to that question. All that it takes is for one interview that is competency-based where they ask you specifics of that skill, or for proof that you actually possess it, and you're done for. A recruiter or even the individual making the hiring decision will respect you more for being honest and direct. Stating that while you may not possess that specific skill, you've had experience in X, Y, or Z that can easily be adapted to make up for what they're looking for. Make sure that your information contained on your CV is 100% honest and accurate, and that it's as up to date as possible. You may have just finished working on a six-month project that is in a similar field as the client's requirements, but there's no point in mentioning it to them during the interview if it wasn't included in your original document.

Is This Really What You Want?

One of the final questions in this section is to be blatantly honest with yourself. You've now been able to see your strengths and limitations laid out bare before you. You know what your interests are and what's likely to make you happy. At the same time, the obvious is likely to make you less happy or desperately unhappy. This was mentioned in an earlier chapter—are you wanting to make this move for the right reasons? If you are doing it for a personal reason, because you don't get along with a work colleague or because you aren't crazy about your boss, remember that individuals change positions all the time—they get promoted, they relocate. Your current situation may not always be there. What's making you miserable at the moment could be as a result of the way you've chosen to view things from your own perspective. Have you stopped to take a look in the mirror to determine whether there's anything that you could be doing to contribute to the situation?

I'll leave this as a personal example: I was once freelancing for one of the most narcissistic management teams I have ever had the displeasure of working with. Instead of going with the flow and reminding myself that I was actually working for myself as a freelancer and could leave at any time, I totally allowed them to get under my skin. They made every waking moment spent in their offices sheer hell until I finally came to my senses and realized that there would be nothing I could do to ever change who they were. I could present strategies until I was blue in the face, I could implement as much staff training, as others before me had attempted to do and failed, but I needed to accept that I could not assume the responsibility for their business decisions. My role in the organization was only a consulting role. Don't get me wrong; I take consulting with businesses extremely seriously, which is probably why I took their refusal to consider any strategic changes as a personal affront. Instead, I should have saved myself months of hand-wringing frustration by arriving at the conclusion way earlier that narcissists seldom see the faults within themselves. Everyone else is always to blame for their failure. I should have just accepted this the third or fourth time around, rather than trying to save something that was ultimately unsalvageable.

Chapter 4: Improving Your Skills

"The truth is that our finest moments are most likely to occur when we are feeling deeply uncomfortable, unhappy, or unfulfilled. For it is only in such moments, propelled by our discomfort, that we are likely to step out of our ruts and start searching for different ways or truer answers."

~ M. Scott Peck

Developing our skills is one of the ways you can make yourself more marketable and prepared for a change in your choice of career. This chapter is going to cover various ways to improve your current skills and possibly develop new ones for a change in career.

Having investigated what's currently available in the industries you're interested in, or possibly even within companies you would like to work for, you've hopefully been able to narrow your next career choices down to a couple of possibilities.

Identify Why You Really Want to Move

According to the Joblist's Midlife Career Crisis report, there are only a number of reasons why people really want to change jobs, especially mid-career. These are listed in order of importance:

- 47% are looking for more money

- 39% are suffering from burnout because of work related stress
- 37% would like to enjoy a better work-life balance
- 25% were looking for a new challenge, and
- 23% admitted they were no longer passionate about their work.

The same survey revealed that most people were happier once they made the career move. They reported as follows:

- 77% were happier
- 75% identified as being more satisfied
- 69% claimed to be more fulfilled with their work, and
- 65% reported being less stressed out.

Those who changed careers also reported earning way more than they did previously (Joblist Blog, 2019).

Before taking the plunge and applying for any of the positions, it's time to consider whether you have the right skills to perform the necessary work. We refer to this as your skill set. This is a collection of skills, talents, and abilities that you have either learned, or they've come to you naturally. They are essential in performing tasks necessary for any position. They are sometimes defined as the group of abilities and skills that may be linked to our interests. And they allow us to complete our tasks in a professional manner.

Examples of skills could be performing difficult calculations, professional writing, listening, and the ability to understand technical concepts or to explain these to others in such a way that they can understand them. Some skills are more obvious, such as being able to operate specific computer programs. These could range from accounting software to specific design applications used to create intricate 3D designs.

How To Identify Your Skills

Discover what you thrive on doing. These are usually the things that you enjoy doing and you can probably do them without too much effort. Do you enjoy doing research, putting presentations together, sharing information with others, or capturing data on spreadsheets? These are just a few examples of what you could really enjoy doing.

When are you praised? Think about times when you are usually praised for doing something really well? What is it? This is probably one of your current skills that you may not even be considering as a skill.

Evaluate Your Current Skill Set

Take the time to evaluate how different your current skills are from the skills necessary in the new position. Make a comprehensive list of both hard and soft skills; this will give you a much clearer image of what you need to be doing or where you need to be going to find the skills necessary.

From all the research conducted, create the following lists:

Hard Skills Necessary Owned

Hard Skills Currently

Soft Skills Necessary Owned

Soft Skills Currently

Hybrid Skills Currently Owned

Hybrid Skills

Do you possess any hybrid skills? These are skills that can be used as a combination of hard and soft skills that make you good at completing a specific profession. An example of this may be communication skills, which are actually a soft skill. When you combine this skill in being able to resolve a customer's problem or query, or being able to close a business deal successfully, that's actually a hard skill that supports the ability to conclude business transactions.

Job-specific skills are those that are necessary to successfully perform a particular job. Having a medical degree and all other relevant practical experience necessary will qualify you to be able to practice medicine. However, having a medical license won't help you to practice law!

Transferable Skills

What skills are you currently using that could easily be transferred and applied in the new position? What are transferable skills? These are the skills that you need for most jobs despite the job title. They include things like basic computer skills and communicating effectively with others in a face-to-face environment, as well as over the telephone. It may even refer to your ability to be able to communicate using emails or other forms of technology. They are skills you use daily that would be applicable to most positions.

Soft Skills

Maybe the skills you need are what we refer to as soft skills. These include things like:

- Management of others
- Interpersonal skills
- Communication
- Presentation skills
- Leadership skills
- Effective time management
- Problem solving
- Being a team player
- Diversity management

Soft skills can often be improved through short courses and are normally applicable in almost every position. These are able to be crossed over or utilized in new careers once you determine how they need to be adapted.

Hard Skills

Hard skills are displayed through physically completing the work required in the workplace and can be easily proven or disproven as being something you're able to do. Hard skills can be developed through inhouse training or finding a mentor who possesses these skills and is prepared to assist you develop them for yourself. A mentor is a great way to go because they are going to motivate you and encourage you to develop the skills on your own. Having a mentor is better than attending a class at a community college for a couple of hours a week or completing an online certification. Better still, if you can combine the two processes, you stand a much better chance of gaining the hard skills you need.

How Do You Go About Developing New Skills?

Be specific about what you want to change and why. You must be able to nail this down into something tangible and realistic before you even begin to work on it. It's more than just wanting the additional skill. You need to be specific about how it's going to lead you to securing the job that you think you want.

Keep a record of how satisfied you are in your current position. This needs to be kept daily and if there's anything that seems to be repetitive or recurring, write it down. You will be amazed that sometimes those things that seem to be major irritations are actually minor irritations and can often be resolved.

Look for places where you can intern or volunteer for free. This will give you a much better idea of whether this is something that you really want to be doing for the remainder of your career.

Do You Need Further Studies?

Do any of these skills require additional education from a formal institute such as a college or university? If there are skills you don't possess yet that are critical to performing on par in your new vocation, find a way to gain these skills before you start applying for new positions. How can you build on these skills until they are solid enough to include on your resume? It's also not enough to be able to include these skills on your resume; you actually need to be able to use them or apply them to a work environment if you want to be considered for a new position. You want these skills to add enough value to your resume to make you a viable candidate. In other words, you need to be able to apply the skills in your work situation.

Who Do I Know?

Are there ways you can learn and develop these skills where you are in your current position? Do you know of someone in your current workplace who possesses the skills that you require who may be prepared to tutor you after hours or in their spare time? Can you apply for a study loan through your current employer for you to obtain these qualifications through a reputable training institution? These requests may be met with some resistance, especially if your employer realizes that you want to profit off of their financial assistance only to resign for another position. If there are departments within your organization that do what you are wanting to do, you may have an easier time convincing management as to why you would like to increase your knowledge, or gain new skills in an area that's not associated with your current position.

Can I Leverage Off My Present Company?

Speak with the training department within your current organization to see whether there are inhouse or external training courses that you may be included in. These could be anything from short courses that cover smaller sections of the overall training you require, to extended training off-site with third-party training institutions. The point is to be looking for the best possible training that's going to provide you with the right skill set. Does your company perhaps cover the cost of becoming certified, or offer other work-related skill-building activities? Check off the various skills necessary for the position you're interested in, against those you already possess. Include each set of skills whether they're hard skills, or soft skills, transferable skills, or hybrid skills. You may possess more of these than you initially believe.

Other Ways To Improve Your Current Skills

Look for feedback from those closest to you in a working environment regarding what they believe to be your strengths and weaknesses. Ask those who know you well enough, but who aren't going to be biased. After all, you are looking for honest answers. Take their feedback seriously and see whether there are areas that you can look to improve on that will also influence your current skills positively.

Contact those already working in the industry you're interested in. Ask them whether they are free for a coffee or a phone call to discuss what they do. When you communicate with them, ask them for both the benefits and negative side of the industry they're in. You need to get a broad overall picture, rather than just considering that a change in career is going to bring you sunshine and roses.

Look Online

If you have a huge gap between the skills you have and the skills you need, it may help to search for online courses with places like Coursera, Udemy, and/or Skillshare. It may also be worthwhile searching for one-day training seminars in your area, or weekend classes. This is especially vital when you need additional hard skills to be able to make the transition into a new career. Are there bridging courses available that can work with your current training and qualifications and allow you certain credits for the skills you already have? This could potentially shorten your study time fairly extensively. This may mean registering for part-time studies through an online institution (university or college) and learning to manage your time effectively. Working and studying requires dedication and commitment because you're juggling different balls in the air constantly. You cannot allow either your current work or your studies to suffer, but you need to be able to separate them from each other.

Setting SMART Goals

Indeed recommends developing these skills using the following techniques:

Identify what it is that you want to achieve and then set SMART goals to help you get there. SMART is an acronym for the words:

Specific: how do each of the goals you've identified fit into the overall picture that you're trying to achieve? Have you defined them so they're clear enough for you to be working towards? If you cannot visualize your goal from what you have identified and written down, it's not specific enough.

Measurable: you need to have your goal broken down into bite-size pieces so you can measure your progress when working toward its achievement. As you reach each of these milestones, you can mark these off and celebrate your achievement.

Achievable: when you specify your goals, you need to be certain that they are achievable. Setting a goal for yourself to aim towards achieving when you know that it will be an impossible task is only going to frustrate you. You want these goals to motivate you and get you moving in the morning.

Relevant: how does this goal apply to your current role, or the role you're hoping to move into? This is something that should always be front of your mind. You need to have a reason for doing what you are doing, otherwise you are just wasting your own time and energy.

Timed: set a specific timeframe for when you would like this goal achieved by. This will include both a start and end date, as well as various check-in markers along the way to ensure that you are able to mark each of these off along the way (Indeed, 2019).

Other Access to Knowledge

Other ways to gain additional knowledge could be through audiobooks, community forums, or articles that are relevant to the industry you're looking to move into. Communities on Facebook or LinkedIn could assist you in finding those groups closest to you, and these will be able to notify you of any special events or training taking place near you. This is a great way to network, meeting up with key influencers in the industry, as well as learning more through proper accredited training. It's important to ensure that the institution or entity you are going to study through will provide you with the right training. Material should be as up to date as possible; you don't want to invest in a training program that has outdated material. It's better to spend a little extra with an accredited institution to receive the training you need to do the job.

Your studies are probably going to set you back financially for as long as it takes to requalify. Starting off at the bottom of a new career will have a similar effect. Look for something you already know how to do that you could possibly offer on a freelance basis or as a side gig to supplement your income while you transition into your new position.

Skills Every Company Needs

Forbes lists the following transferable skills as top of the list when it comes to any new position. When job seekers can identify these trends across all vacancies, they will be able to identify which of these skills they need to be working on. In total, there are seven of them, and just as anything in life, the more boxes you're able to tick off, the more valuable you are to an organization. The skills are:

Communication: how effective are your communication skills within your own organization, as well as with those externally? Communication covers a broad spectrum including spoken, written, verbal, and non-verbal communication. Are you also able to pick up on non-verbal cues of people in your team, making you better at communicating effectively to meet their needs and not just your own?

Creativity: how creative are you in resolving problems and coming up with new ideas to implement or revolutionize an industry? This is not always about being able to draw or design, or being good with developing something out of a raw material, instead, it's being able to look at new ways to manage problems and coming up with solutions that may present an entirely new approach to doing business.

Critical Thinking: can you make use of critical thinking techniques where you can make connections between what needs to happen? It's being able to think logically to solve problems and presenting workable solutions by joining those ideas together that not only make the most sense, but could save the organization time and money.

Leadership: can you lead multi-functional teams of individuals, or smaller departments towards the achievement of corporate goals? Are you able to obtain their buy-in from an early stage so they support you in your decision-making process? Leadership is not always about leading from the front; occasionally it means being able to work alongside your team and keeping them motivated.

Multitasking: referring back to the juggling act earlier. Are you able to keep multiple projects or tasks in the air simultaneously while keeping your finger on the pulse of exactly what's happening? If something needs your attention and to be managed specifically, can you do this without losing focus of other expectations?

Teamwork: are you able to work together with multi-dimensional, cross-functional teams? Can you do so effectively, accepting each individual who has a different cultural background and sharing mutual respect in order to produce high quality work?

Technical: do you have the necessary technical skills that are relevant to the task at hand? Are you able to complete these assignments because you have the right skills to do so? Are each of these skills completed to the best of your ability (Yate, 2018)?

Chapter 5:
What Can You Still Do While In Your Job?

"The biggest mistake that you can make is to believe that you are working for someone else... The driving force of a career must come from the individual. Remember: Jobs are owned by the company; you own your career!

~ Earl Nightingale

During your transition period, there are things that you are still able to do that are productive and can help you move forward. This chapter will discuss important things you can do while in your current occupation that will help you with your career change in the future.

Consider Remaining In The Same Industry

If you have been working in the same industry for an extended period of time, you probably have an extensive knowledge of how your industry works. This could be beneficial to you, as well as any organization in your current industry that hires you. There's a reason why most job postings require previous experience, it's simply because you will be able to save them valuable resources in having to cross-train you or re-train you in a new industry. Each industry has their own set of unique standards or industry norms and having to re-learn these all over again takes time and resources.

Consider moving laterally within your current industry. This could allow you to make use of the industry knowledge you already have, e.g. if you are a warehouse manager for a large distribution chain and have grown tired of the warehouse environment, you could consider a move to external sales for the same industry or you could look at moving into a procurement role within the distribution industry at a corporate head office level. If you are a programmer who is tired of programming, consider a lateral move into technical sales or project management. Once you begin looking within your current industry, it may just surprise you exactly how many positions there are that may be exactly what you are looking for.

Repair Relationships Before Moving

You've probably heard the term, "Don't burn your bridges." It's especially true when choosing to remain within the same industry. We've discussed that it's never a good idea to leave things until it's too late before considering a move. This means being able to identify what you want to be doing as quickly as possible and then doing something about it daily. Kathy Caprino recommends mending all the fences that may potentially be broken before you decide to leave. This will leave your reputation intact (especially if you're planning on moving laterally within the same industry.) Employees don't realize how small industries are, and if you're leaving a company on bad terms, the word is likely to spread. In addition, those interviewing you or making the hiring decision are likely to complete reference checks and when done in the right way, they are able to get this information out of the referee. You want to ensure that there's nothing left to be said, other than positive things.

Proactive Things to Do

There are so many proactive things that you can do while still working for your current employer that will benefit you in the long run. Each of these are going to take substantial work and effort, and there's no such thing as waving a magic wand and hoping for the best. Delve back into your past (sometimes going back as far as your teenage years.) What did you really enjoy doing at the time? Did you enjoy poetry or writing, were you on the debate team, or did you play sports? What part of your social experiences from your youth really excited you? Maybe you were one of those kids who enjoyed pulling things apart and putting them back together again to see how they worked. If this describes you, you're actually in good company—that's exactly how Henry Ford got started. He was given a pocket watch as a birthday gift from his father on his 13th birthday. Being interested in all things technical and mechanical, he pulled it apart and put it back together again. Young Henry needed to understand how it worked. This early passion was never lost on him; instead, it spurred him on to build the first automobile and become a global force to be reckoned with.

Capriano recommends reconnecting with your younger self, investigating those things that you were passionate about in your youth. Some of these may be exactly what you're currently missing out on, or craving. Are there areas in your current position that you could try to incorporate these interests to make your job more exciting for you? It may be worthwhile to consider some of your earlier positions. Which did you absolutely love? And what were the things that you loved about them? Which did you hate? And what parts of the position did you loathe? This exercise takes a lot of personal introspection and cannot be done in a hurry. Remember that this is your future you're talking about and if you're already in the middle of your career, chances are this will be one of your final major changes. Can you afford to get it wrong?

Take the time, make lists of things you enjoyed versus things you didn't enjoy. Once you've completed your lists, ask whether there's anything else. Information is power, especially when it comes to what motivates you and what will make you passionate about getting up in the morning.

Even in your current career, try to avoid all those things that you absolutely hate. These are the parts of our career that drain the very lifeblood out of us and make us feel exhausted (before we even get into work in the mornings). Are there areas that you don't enjoy that could be reassigned to other members of your team? Maybe someone else loves doing spreadsheets and pivot tables, and all the number crunching drives you insane? Small tweaks in our current positions can occasionally make them bearable, or even enjoyable again. There must have been some reason for you taking on this role in the first place. Discover what drew you to your current position.

As a career coach, Capriano spends a lot of time with her clients doing exactly this. Analyzing previous positions against their current position, looking for patterns, themes in their work history, and problem areas that are creating barriers for them to either move up the corporate ladder or achieving the goals they set themselves. Other barriers or roadblocks are easily overcome which is why it's important to know WHY you want to move out of your current position in the first place. Capriano does mention however that everyone deserves being able to live the life of their dreams, which includes working in the position that they really want. It's not just some Hollywood fantasy, or something entitled to a select few. Instead, it should be everyone's right to be able to work in the career of their choice.

What You Should Do NOW

Look for as many ways as you can to broaden your knowledge and skill set that will support the career of your choosing. We've covered this extensively in the previous chapter, but some other pointers include:

Set aside a set amount of time daily for improving your skills. This could involve online learning, speaking with those who already possess these skills, or broadening your current network. This you could do by joining various forums or associations that are associated with the skills you need. Try to find a colleague who is prepared to show you the ropes after hours, volunteer to work on a project or try job shadowing. If you are planning to job shadow a particular position, try to shadow several different individuals to give you a broad overview of what's involved. The reason for this is that everyone works differently, and what you may not enjoy by watching one individual may not necessarily be the same with several others.

Keep A Record of Accomplishments

We all accomplish things on a regular basis that are often memorable at the time, and they make us really good at our jobs. These accomplishments should be accurately recorded so they can be included on your resume. Companies looking to hire are looking for people who will bring value to their organization, and being able to identify strategic highlights and accomplishments in your current career could be the difference between being hired or not. Add these accomplishments to your resume and keep it up to date.

Connect with Colleagues on Social Media

Make use of professional social media sites such as LinkedIn, or business-related groups on Facebook. Keep abreast of changes in the industry so you remain informed and up to date. There are many other blogs or social media influencers that you can connect with to receive regular material from them to keep you motivated, or to join a unique platform where knowledge about the industry of your choice can be delivered directly into your inbox. Being active on sites such as LinkedIn can introduce you to other individuals in the industry you're interested in and may provide you with a springboard to key introductions that can change your career.

Do Your Job Well

While you are still in your current position, do your work to the very best of your ability. One of the worst things you could do is committing career suicide by adopting a lazy attitude towards your work or doing whatever is required with a half-hearted approach. This doesn't go unnoticed. It will be much better for you in the long-term for you to give your work your best possible effort, right until the day you leave. Remember that you will have a career reference attached to this position, even if you're moving in another direction entirely. You still need to rely on a reference from your manager, or other executives within the company that you're leaving. A bad reference, or one that states that your work over the last few months took a nosedive is not going to do your future career prospects any good. Always put your very best foot forward; it's worth it in the long run.

Appoint an Accountant

You've already crunched some of the numbers on your own, but it's now time to get in touch with a professional. Speak with your accountant about your intentions to move and what it will mean to you and your family financially. Your accountant may join you in your research, or they may even provide their own additional financial information that you had not considered. Remember that for you this is an emotional decision. You have come to a crossroad in your career and don't feel like you can continue where you are at present. Your accountant is going to consider all aspects realistically and without emotion. They will be able to give you the hard facts of what is necessary for you to be able to make a final decision, especially when it's going to hit your pocket where it hurts most.

There are some vital pieces of information that you should be entrusting your financial consultant or accountant with. Can you afford to leave your current position? Can you afford to survive without work, or how long can you afford to survive without work? Can you afford to restart your career at an entry level position? If not, what is it going to take for you to be able to survive and what plan do you have in place to get there?

Consider Roadblocks

From where you are now to where you want to be is going to take some serious work, unless you have a pile of transferable skills that can reposition you in a similar mid-career position in a new industry. Some of these challenges that you may need to overcome are as follows:

Lack of industry or relevant experience

Despite this, you may have been able to rack up some time volunteering or working with projects where some of these skills and talents have been necessary. This should clearly be indicated on your resume, as well as your willingness to learn.

Insufficient skills to be considered seriously

The amount of skills you have acquired may still not be enough for the potential employer to take you seriously. Consider ways to convince them just how serious you are. This may be a good time to highlight and discuss your transferable skills that you would be able to easily apply to the new position.

Graduates with qualifications

This will always present as a problem when changing careers mid-stream. It will always be the employer's prerogative to hire young, fresh, blood that is leaving the hallowed halls of an educational institution. For some reason, organizations feel that it's easier to mold these candidates while considering older candidates more set in their ways.

Candidates with experience

This is always going to be a genuine threat to the hiring process. Normally these candidates come as the full package with both qualifications and experience. The only downside to them is they may be looking for a much higher salary as compensation for the same work. The other downside for employers is that if they're looking to leave their current employer now, what's to say that they're not going to want to make another move again in a hurry?

High-risk candidate

Just as much as the previous candidates could be perceived as high-risk, you too could be viewed in the same light. There are several reasons why a prospective employer may be wary of hiring you. You are making a major career move mid-career. What's to say that you're not just having a midlife crisis, or you're actually going to fit into the new environment? It may be that you don't enjoy the new position after all, despite all your volunteering, job shadowing and discussing the change with industry experts.

Lack of support from family and/or friends

This is potentially one of the most challenging or difficult obstacles to overcome. If you don't have the support in your new position that you need, you are going to find those down days when you really need a listening ear, especially difficult to work through.

These are only a few obstacles that you may be faced with during your career transition. It's worth taking the time and trying to brainstorm as many possible objections as you can so you can prepare for them. Being prepared for what you may face is half the battle to actually winning the war.

Chapter 6:
Finding The Opportunities

"Many of us have created lives that give very little support for experimentation. We believe that answers already exist out there, independent of us. What if we invested more time and attention to our own experimentation? We could focus our efforts on solutions that work uniquely for us."

~ Margaret Wheatley

Up to now we have spent a lot of time investigating what skills and expertise are necessary for you to move into this exciting new career. This chapter will discuss how you can find and land a job in the career that you've set your sights on. These steps are as crucial to get right, if not even more so, because this will be exactly what the recruiter or agency sees first. In this chapter we are going to concentrate on getting your resume into top shape so that you stand the best possible chance at landing your dream job.

Updating Your Resume and Cover Letter

Why is it so important to have an updated resume, and cover letter? This is possibly one of the biggest mistakes that all career-seekers make. They believe that their "universal" resume is suitable for all job applications, and this is also normally backed up with a fairly bland generic cover letter. The truth is that the resume you send out for specific jobs needs to be geared specifically to that particular job. And while I can hear massive sighs in the background, believe me, this minor tweak to your resume will potentially make the difference between whether the recruiter or hiring manager simply scans past your resume, or whether they stop long enough to scan through it.

Understanding the numbers when it comes to recruiting may give you an indication as to why some resumes simply aren't even considered and end up in the trash before you've even begun.

Consider a day in the life of a hiring manager or recruiter (and it doesn't matter whether they're inhouse or agency). Most are working multiple job postings simultaneously. Let's put a really low number on this and say that they are working on between five to seven postings at any given time (and this is being conservative).

Hints When Working With Hiring Managers/Recruiters

Hint 1

They are updating job portals online (normally multiple portals to attract the best possible candidates) and may even be scouring platforms as part of a proactive search, or with the intention of head-hunting. Platforms that are ideal for this are social media platforms such as LinkedIn, or whichever platforms the recruiter has access to that is going to allow them to physically search for candidates using keywords.

Hint 2

Depending on what their search turns up, they may or may not upload a job posting on the various job boards. If you have already applied for one of these positions and you happen to see exactly the same advertisement through the same agency on another job portal, don't apply again. All that this does is fill the recruiter's inbox and if your resume is detailed enough and covers all the bases, they do not need it more than once.

Hint 3

Follow all of the instructions in the online job ad. If it asks you to quote a reference number, quote the reference number. If it has a recruiter's name, use it. If it asks for a cover letter, send a professional cover letter that is directly positioned to that particular job. Do not send a generic cover letter; recruiters receive hundreds of these each day and are inclined to immediately skip past your application without even looking at your resume. I know that it sounds cruel, but if you multiply the five to seven job listings that the recruiter is currently working on by an average of 150-200 resumes per job posting per day, you can begin to see how the numbers begin to take over. For a recruiter, it's survival of the fittest. They want to know that you can follow orders.

Hint 4

Keep your cover letter brief and to the point, but cover all the important information and keywords used in the advertisement as they are applicable to you.

Hint 5

Be honest at all times. Recruiters can also pick up whether you are just using verbiage to make it sound as though you know what the job is about, or to prove that you are superior. This is yet another huge no-no! They want to know that if they bring you in for an interview, you are not going to sit there trying to "lord it over them."

There are loads of other hints with regards to your cover letter, and we are going to provide you with some sample cover letters to follow that you could apply to any position as long as you remember to tailor them to the job. You want to be professional, succinct and to the point, and highlight the areas of your expertise as they pertain to the position you are applying for. Basically, your cover letter should be a few sentences or brief paragraphs explaining why the recruiter should meet with you and what makes you an ideal candidate for the job.

Your Resume

Apart from all your relevant contact information (and yes, people do leave their contact information off their resumes), your resume should also be as short and to the point as possible. Highlight any skills that you have that you can apply to the new position as part of a brief introduction and provide them with a reason why you believe you are both qualified and suitable for serious consideration.

Place a specific emphasis on transferable skills, as well as hybrid skills that you can make use of. Highlight roles that you have had in the past, or achievements that indicate you're well qualified for a change in roles. If you know who the company is, it's important to express your passion for the company, their culture, ethics, or whatever other reason you feel drawn to have applied for the role. You can also express your interest in the position and explain your reason behind wanting to change.

Please find the following templates of a sample cover letter, as well as a sample resume. These will entirely depend on the type of role that you are applying for. Beneath the sample documents are some do's and don'ts that include common mistakes candidates make with their cover letters or resumes that will cost them a chance at the job every time.

Sample Resumes

You are responding to an advertisement on an online job portal such as Indeed, Glassdoor, or Monster, each a reputable international job board that operates globally across all business spectrums. Before you can physically search for openings on any of these sites you will need to register with them. This process is not a lengthy one, and usually allows you to typically provide a few job titles that you are interested in. For the best results, try to leave as many of the search parameters as broad as possible. For example, if you are looking to stay in the same industry, select the boxes of job titles you are interested in. Setting your alerts to daily, weekly, or monthly for each will keep your inbox buzzing with job openings that may meet your background and expertise. Remember your transferable skills and your hybrid skills? This is where these features are. You will be asked to either upload your resume or complete their online format.

> **_Sidebar_**: *If you upload your own resume on any job portal, please go back through their online format to make certain that your information has populated their headings correctly. Everyone selects a different format for their resume in an attempt to stand out and provide themselves with the best possible chance of being noticed. Do this with words, rather than having a document either incomplete, or with the wrong data. Focus on providing clear information on your skills. Look for keywords that most of these positions in the industry use in their advertisements and populate your resume with these keywords and phrases, making your application one that will receive attention.*

Choose a functional layout for your resume, or a combination between a conventional and functional resume. Examples below include a functional resume and a combination resume that you can use as guidelines to create the best possible resume for yourself.

While there are many different types of resumes you can put together to showcase your talents and abilities, we are going to focus on two that will be specifically beneficial. The first is a basic, one-page resume that is only going to provide the bare essential information. This is not recommended for a career change; however, you do get hiring managers and recruiters who specifically ask for this type of resume, so it is in your best interests to know how to create this single page document.

Single Page Career Summary Resume

Name

Contact number

Email Address

LinkedIn URL (direct link)

Objective

State a brief objective of what you are trying to achieve.

Career Summary and Professional Profile

One or two brief paragraphs outlining what you have been doing. This is usually written in the third person. This may list soft skills that you possess that contribute towards your success in the workplace.

Key Competencies

List each of these in bullet point format beneath each other. This would include transferable skills as well as hybrid skills that you can use across industries. You must be able to substantiate each of these.

Keep adding under the bulleted list until you mention all your competencies.

Key Achievements (or Accomplishments)

List each key achievement under a bulleted list along with as much data as possible.

Continue with this list until you've captured all your achievements.

Employment History

Dates of service   Company   Designation

Follow the same format until you have included all of your work history.

Education

Institution, qualification, year graduated

Complete brief list until all relevant qualifications are included.

Certificates

Available on request.

References

Available on request.

Functional Resume

The following sample resume is an example of what you should send if you are in the sales and marketing environment. If you are in IT or accounting, it should obviously be drawn up focusing on those key areas. Remember that this is purely an example.

Name and Surname

Email address

Contact number

Professional social media profile (LinkedIn) as a clickable link

Career Profile

Present yourself in the third person and provide a basic background into the work you have done in the past or the industries you've been involved with.

This introduction should be one or two paragraphs long and verbiage used should professionally highlight your strengths. This is the first glimpse the recruiter or hiring manager gets of you, so it should be strong enough to make them want to meet with you.

Achievements

List specific achievements in bullet form, short and to the point, but provide all the information. (If you were part of a multinational, cross-functional team that secured a multi-billion-dollar tender within a short space of time, this is where this information belongs). Provide specific numbers, duration of project, and your particular role.

Continue in the same fashion by listing each of your major achievements one below the other until you have listed all of them. If you've worked internationally, this is where you showcase this connection.

Sales/Marketing

List key highlights of your career under bullet points. Once again, remember to include facts, figures, and vital information. Continue with these bullet points until you have no more information to give.

Repeat the process for any of the following headings

that are relevant to your industry and the career you have had (transferable and hybrid skills).

Communications

Each sub-heading should include key information regarding experience and key career highlights below.

Public Relations

Advertising

Media

Employment History

Here you are going to provide a list of where you have worked, with dates. Minimal information is included here, not even your reasons for leaving. This will look something like this:

Date to present   Current Designation
                         Current Company
                         What do they do

Date to date	Previous Designation
	Name of Company
	What do they do

(Repeat the process until you have gone back approximately 10 years.)

Education and Qualifications

Qualification
Institution, date

Qualification
Institution, date

Qualification
Institution, date

Certificates
Available upon request

References
Available upon request

Do's for Your Resume

- Lay your resume out as cleanly, crisply, and clearly as possible.
- Explain the why behind your career change, as well as experience that you have had that's brought you to this decision.
- Highlight what you can do for the company, not what you are excited to learn from them.
- Write a resume objective. Use this space to make it clear how your former career has provided you with the skills you need for your new field.
- A functional resume is often the best choice for someone switching careers since it puts the focus squarely on the relevant skills and experience.
- Add a skills section.
- Recruiters or hiring managers might not see familiar job titles or responsibilities from their industry. Leave out ALL unnecessary information.
- Watch for jargon. Terms in your old industry may be different from the new one.
- Focus on quality, not quantity.

Don'ts for Resumes

- Use multiple fonts or choose a font that's difficult to read. The best resumes are balanced with the right spacing and fonts. The information is neatly presented and makes sense.

- Stay away from multiple colors, even if you have used a resume template from the Internet or your word processing package.

- Remove all unnecessary pages, such as a title page that just has your name on. This information is repetitive, and you're trying to avoid the hiring manager having to sift through reams of paper to find what's relevant to the position you're applying for.

- Do not attach any certificates of qualification or references unless specifically requested as part of the application process.

Sample Cover Letter

Address cover letters to the person by name if it is stipulated in the job opening, or if you've been referred. Addressing individuals formally is the most correct way.

Date

Dear Sir/Madam, (or, To whom it may concern)

Subject: Your ad for Technical Sales Agent (TSA1234)

In response to the above ad advertised on Indeed.com on dd/mm/yyyy, please find my application attached.

I have X amount of years' experience working within a technical sales environment. and my expertise includes:

(list expertise in short bullet points)

I am available to discuss your opportunity further and would welcome either telephonic communication or via email as indicated below.

Thank you for taking the time to consider my application. I look forward to hearing from you at your earliest convenience.

Kind regards

John Brown

(555) 267 1234

johnbrown22@gmail.com

Do's for Cover Letters

- State the reference to the job, the title of the job, and the job board you saw the posting on, as well as the date.

- Provide a very brief synopsis of your skills, any specific achievements that you have that will be beneficial to the position they have advertised, and why you are a good match for the job.

- Indicate that your resume is attached for their perusal.

- Thank them for taking the time to go through your resume.

- End off the cover letter with your full name, as well as your contact details (a mobile number, and your email address).

Don'ts for Cover Letters

- Don't address the individual as if you know them. Always remain professional and polite, but not overly friendly.

- Don't use abbreviated verbiage that would normally be used when chatting with a friend over social media. This is career suicide for any professional role, and it's something that professional recruiters sift out immediately into the trash without even looking at your actual resume.

- Double check your cover letter for spelling and grammar. There's nothing worse than these being glaringly obvious in a cover letter already. The recruiter automatically assumes that the resume is going to be exactly the same. Result = the trash can.

- This may be stating the obvious, but don't forget to attach your resume to the cover letter that you're about to send off.

- Don't change fonts and colors or add pictures to make it look "pretty." Professional recruiters don't have time for "pretty," unless you are actually applying for a graphic design job, in which instance, attach a separate, professional portfolio along with your resume, or indicate that this is available should they so wish.

- Don't leave off vital information regarding the job opening. This is how recruiters sift through thousands of responses each day and are able to file resumes into different categories. Without it, especially when coming from another industry, it's difficult and frustrating for the recruiter to "guess" which opening you are applying for.

Networking

While you may have managed to develop an extensive network through your old career, this network is not going to be of much use to you in your new position. You need to find ways to establish an entirely different network that can benefit you in your change of career. So how do you go about making this transition?

Make a list of everyone you know who is currently involved in the new industry or has an affiliate role with the new industry. An example of this may be that you're looking at getting into event planning, and you need to connect with various venues that could be potentially utilized for functions, conferences, team building events, or getaways. Although you may not have the physical contacts, you may know of someone who supplies them specialized seafood. By connecting with this supplier, you may be able to gain access to a list of potential contacts, especially for networking.

Be sure to ask your contact whether you may mention them by name as having referred you to them. There is usually not a problem if your contact is on good business terms with them. This may allow you access to begin your very own network that may be leveraged for the business that you are after.

Your previous network may have worked well for you, with most of them being supportive and acting as cheerleaders as you grew in your career. Because of this, not all of them are going to be as supportive of you wanting to jump ship and change careers mid-stream. Be aware of this and keep an eye out for any of them who may actually be willing to sabotage the career shift purely because they don't agree with it. In this instance you may need to change networks and gently cut ties with your old network in favor of those who are going to support you. There are a number of ways to learn to prioritize those in your new network listed below.

Prioritize Contacts in New Network

Alumni (at alma mater)

This may include earlier institutions that you've studied with, as well as those that are more recent. Contact those who are in career guidance or career counseling and see where they are able to direct you. This is one of your most valuable resources and should be nurtured. Before leaving training, you should already be building this network of contacts. If you neglected to do this, get in touch with your classmates and ask them for assistance. You may also be able to find these individuals on your college or university website, or there are often sites and groups dedicated specifically to alumni. LinkedIn could be a great resource for this.

Cheerleaders

Focus on those cheerleaders who are always there for you no matter what. You want these individuals to be aware of what you're doing. These people are your sounding boards when things don't seem to be going your way or are taking longer than you anticipated. Strengthen or maintain the relationships with those who are always positive and look on the bright side of life—those who take the time to listen and motivate you when you're feeling down in the dumps, or in a rut. Do your best to hang onto those who will keep you going even during the rough patches.

If you currently have cheerleaders who appear to be negative and unsupportive of your move, possibly even being openly against it, begin to cut ties with these individuals as they are only going to drag you down with them. You are looking for those individuals who will support you and be behind you no matter what. Don't automatically assume that because you've been long-standing friends with people that they will automatically support your decision to make a major career change in the middle of your career. They are going to assume that you're having a midlife crisis and that it needs to blow over. Remember that they have not gone through the entire career analysis process and don't exactly understand what you are going through or where your head is at right now.

Connectors

Sort through your current list of connectors. The example we used above regarding looking to move into the event planning space and connecting with someone who has loads of contacts in the restaurant venue industry. This is a typical connector. It's someone who has loads of contacts that they can put you in touch with. Some of these are connectors due to the nature of their work (i.e. they know a lot of people in various fields). Many of them are natural connectors due to their outgoing personality, and they simply know a lot of people who know a lot of people. The chances of them being able to introduce you to someone in the right industry is highly probable.

Natural connectors are extremely charismatic. These should be at the top of your list of networkers, next to industry experts, entrepreneurs, and influencers. It's important to these individuals that you remain in contact with them. Often, they are social butterflies and love to be the life and soul of the party, which is what makes them so successful. They are not always going to be available to reach out to you, but given their natures and personalities, they will get back to you. The fact that connectors love people make them extremely valuable as a resource because they tend to have their finger on the pulse of whatever is happening in most industries. They are bound to know key influencers and thought leaders in your new industry. You want to stick close to these within your network; they will be able to do what they do best—connect you to where you need to be.

Entrepreneurs

Making use of entrepreneurs as part of your network would be similar to working with other career changers. Although entrepreneurs will not necessarily be able to help you with a new career, they may be able to provide you with some interesting insights and different perspectives to consider. Entrepreneurs have been part of the startup process before, and as such, they know exactly what it takes to become successful or to get wherever it is that you need to go. They understand the high-risk factor of beginning something new and could potentially be great sounding boards for business advice. Don't discredit them because you're not thinking of venturing into your own business.

Experts

Experts are one of the most important groups for you to be focusing on. They will have connections throughout your new industry in almost every single avenue from recruitment to individuals who may become potential mentors in your new career. You want to nurture and strengthen these relationships without wasting their time. Not only will they be able to introduce you to the right people, but they will also be able to give you industry insights that are not always available to those who aren't in the industry. If you don't have any experts in your new industry, look at developing a relationship with some of them via industry networking events, business breakfasts, conventions, and short training courses or specialist speakers. Reinventing yourself and beginning networking again within a new industry is never easy, but it can prove to be extremely rewarding if you manage to connect with the right people.

Influencers

Influencers are decision-makers in the new industry. Examples of key influencers are recruiters, hiring managers, management on various levels within the new industry, thought leaders, and others. These are the individuals who could at least open a door for you into your new career. Recruiters and hiring managers always have their fingers on the pulse of what's happening in the industry. If they are part of your network, they can assist you from helping you refine your resume to knowing which positions are going to be your best stepping stone to the career of your choice. These recruiters may even be from your old network. Remember that this is a relatively small marketplace and they will know of other recruiters who operate in your new marketplace. Submitting a referral candidate from a recruiter or hiring manager goes a long way to cut through a ton of red tape.

Other Career Changers

Get in touch with others who have transitioned mid-career. You probably know more of these than you realize. They can not only act as cheerleaders when things seem to be going slowly, or they could act as a whole new source of wisdom that has remained untapped to this point. Look for these individuals within your old and new network. The likelihood of them judging you negatively or harshly is minimal, as they have already gone through what you are currently facing right now, so they understand and will be much more likely to offer support.

Potential Employers

Look at hooking up with potential employers at networking meetings and events, and/or via LinkedIn.

Recruiters/Hiring Managers

What about contacting these recruiters and hiring managers directly off of their advertisements, via job portals, and through LinkedIn? Let them know your current skill sets, why you are suited to any of their positions that fall in line with what you're looking for, and what your main career objective is at the moment. It may even be possible for you to send through a copy of your resume and ask them for some honest feedback as to what you can improve on that may help you land the job of your dreams. Tell them what you are trying to accomplish and ask for any assistance they may be able to offer you.

How to Start Networking

Look at Connecting

Does the very word 'networking' make a knot form in your stomach? Or do your palms begin sweating to match the pace that your heart has increased to? Does the thought of approaching strangers almost scare you to death, especially when you're planning on doing it in an industry you know little to nothing about? The easiest way out of this conundrum is to shift your mindset from the traditional "I'm looking to get something out of you" networking approach to "I'm looking forward to meeting up with interesting new people who can share some ideas with me." Your biggest focus should be on connecting with others, rather than looking at them for something you can get out of them.

Be Honest

Honesty is always the best policy and discuss your career shift openly. Discuss your reasons for wanting to make the transition, and also why now. Don't hide anything that could be discovered later and prove to be uncomfortable. Changing careers can be difficult and uncomfortable. Be prepared to discuss these scenarios openly.

Ask Questions About Them

Developing new networks is very much like making new friends, and you should want to find out as much about them as possible. Express a genuine interest in their story and where they've come from, and allow them to open up to you. You will be amazed by what you discover.

Be Specific

During your discussions and interactions, be detailed and specific about what you're asking for. When we are vague, we tend to get vague reactions and responses back from our network. It's easy for us to throw our hands in the air, claiming that networking is not for us, and to throw the towel in regarding meeting anyone new. The main thing with networking is that you're working with people and individuals who are each different, requiring different things from the person they're networking with. As you can tell from the long list of different networking contacts above, you could have very different motives for connecting with each of them. Be clear and specific as to what you expect out of the relationship. You may be pleasantly surprised by how accommodating they can be when they understand exactly what you're looking for.

Respect People's Time

The old saying "time is money" is always true when it comes to networking, and it's important to always respect the time of the person you are seeking help from. Most of these individuals are in high-powered positions and for them, even considering meeting with you is making a sacrifice of part of their day. To them, you are an anomaly and they do not know whether you are worth an investment of their time. The best way to maximize this is to put an agenda in place or have a list of specific questions written down. This not only appears more organized, but it saves you from forgetting anything important during your discussions. You may even want to give them a list of your questions, along with some further dates and times when it may be more convenient to meet up again. Ask them if there are other sources that you can refer to in order to find the information you're after.

Be Prepared to do Research on Your Own

Be prepared to do as much of the work on your own as you can to make the networking process easier for them. Let them know that you're willing to do the work and that you don't expect a free ride from them or their years' worth of experience in an industry that you essentially know very little about.

Have Something of Value to Offer in Return

Find something of value to offer in return for their help. This could be anything from a fruit basket, or flowers, or even an excellent bottle of wine. Maybe it's something simple, like taking them out for a meal. Hopefully with the amount of time you would have spent together, you know them and you should have an idea of their preferences. Offer them something of value for their assistance. If this key individual is offering you employment, however, don't go down this route as this could potentially be seen as a bribe.

Now that you've taken the time to prioritize those on your current network, reach out to those who seem to know a lot of people. Ask them for introductions.

Don't be afraid to get out to different events and just meet interesting people. This could be as simple as meeting someone at the refreshments table and introducing yourself. As uncomfortable as it might be, the baby bird needs to be able to leave the security of its nest once in a while so it can learn to fly.

Exchange information with those you find interesting and set up a suitable date and time to meet up for coffee. Let the process follow through from there. You never know where it's going to lead, as Natasha Stanley describes in her experience meeting up with a business consultant at a networking event. The two clicked instantly, and their "coffee date" a few days later was the beginning of an amazing collaboration. She remembers feeling that it was the furthest thing from any networking experience she'd ever had in the past, yet it was networking. She adds that "networking, when done right, is the single best thing you can do for your career change" (Stanley, n.d.).

Understanding the Recruitment Process

Just by reading the above heading, it becomes crystal clear that recruitment and hiring is just another business process that needs to be followed. One of the most important things that job seekers and career changers need to understand is that throughout this process, there are steps that need to be followed along the way. Each of these steps are generally still managed by people. Although the recruitment and hiring process has changed a great deal over the last few decades with the introduction of advanced technology, it's helped make the world smaller and brought us much closer together. It makes connecting much easier, and both recruiters and candidates are more flexible and open to new ideas and connecting via technology. Interviews can now be conducted remotely, saving time and money, and recruiters can maximize their output because of this. Having said all of this, though, it's still important to remember that you are working with people. All individuals have different quirks and complexities that make them who they are. Recruiters or hiring managers are not better than candidates.

They know their clients better than prospective candidates do, making it easier for them to identify whether the candidate will fit into their organization or not. They are aware of unwritten rules of engagement within the business. Some of these are cultural requirements, dress standards, and codes of conduct and ethics. Some companies even hire a specific "look." It's important not to get too caught up in the details if after the initial meeting the recruiter or hiring manager lets you know that your application has been unsuccessful. Most times, recruiters don't need to provide you with reasons why, but during this career transition phase it may be in your best interest to ask.

This may potentially be the yellow card that is preventing the recruiter from working with you. If it appears that you're being "blocked" before you've even got out of the starting gates, ask them to be direct and honest with you. This may just provide them with the reassurance they need that you are serious about making a move and not just window-shopping. Candidates often use interviews as a means of leveraging their current employers for salary increases, which quickly devolve into a bidding war. This doesn't sit well with potential hiring companies or recruiters, as effectively you've been wasting their time. Make certain that the recruiter understands how serious you are about a change in your career at this point in time.

What You Can Say During an Interview

Switching careers, especially after a lengthy career within another industry, can make you completely lethargic and complacent about the recruitment/interview process. It's worthwhile keeping up to date with those things that you should be saying in an interview.

Before diving into the list, remember to be sincere in the way you communicate anything to the recruiter or hiring manager.

Honesty is always the best policy

Always be honest, even if you're asked some uncomfortable questions. If you were dismissed from your previous employer (or any other employer for that matter, be open and up front about it). The truth will always come out. It's always better for it to come from your lips rather than during a reference process.

Display your knowledge of the client

Let the hiring manager know that you've done your research on the company (if you know who the company is), and you're up to date with the latest trends in the industry. Visit their website, be aware of what's happening in their business. If they're listing on the Stock Exchange, or about to launch a new product, display your enthusiasm towards the forward momentum of the business (remember—be genuine.)

Display Your Passion

Allow the hiring manager to see how passionate you are for the new industry and the career shift. Be prepared to tackle this question as early on in the interview process as you can. This is going to be like the massive elephant in the room, and everyone is going to want explanations about the mid-career shift. Always be prepared with the right answer. This could be anything from having reached a glass ceiling, to being let go as a result of the economic climate, to discovering a new passion. It's best to approach this topic on your own before they do.

Be Positive About Ex-Employers

Never use an interview situation to badmouth your previous company, management, or employer. This never sits well with any hiring manager. What you're doing now will be what you do with them someday. It's just in poor taste. No matter your reasons for leaving your previous company, remain positive about them (even under challenging circumstances). The last thing you want is to start a mudslinging match regarding businesses or management. If you don't have anything nice to say about them, keep quiet.

Highlight Your Value

Be positive about the value that you have to bring to the new position. Share this information with the hiring manager and provide examples of how you have applied these skills in your previous position. We are referring to soft skills, hard skills, transferable skills, and hybrid skills here. Identify skills that you have been using in your previous position. Provide solid examples of how you have made use of these skills before and how you could possibly apply them to the new position.

Be Prepared

Attend the interview prepared. Take along work samples to display your ability to do the work. Ensure all your certifications and qualifications are with you in case they ask for these at the time. These are proof that you have the relevant training to be able to do the work required. If you don't have any fixed experience in performing certain tasks, yet you have proven competence through recent training, take some time to put together some mock-ups or examples of work for them to assess your ability.

If you are moving into an online marketing role, take samples of several blog articles that you may have written for them to assess. Having all this extra material with you will build on your proof of being able to do the job.

Be Comfortable with Limitations

Don't expect to be able to do everything required of you in your new position immediately. You are going to go through a growth phase. As such, it will take you some time to get on board and on track with where you need to be. Allow yourself the time to learn and perfect your specialization within your new role. Don't expect to know everything immediately. The reality is that nobody within every industry enters the industry knowing everything. Be prepared for a learning curve; it's a natural progression. Think back to when you first began in your previous career; it wasn't an expectation then and it certainly won't be an expectation now.

Highlight Transferable Skills

Before attending the interview, take the time to sit with a list of skills that you made use of in your previous position versus skills that you're going to require now. Write everything down so you're prepared to compare and provide actual examples of when you've had to use these skills for example in management or having to work through conflict resolution successfully with other team members. Be able to connect the skills you're using at the moment with skills that are required for the new position. Explain how these skills can benefit the new position.

How Are You Planning to Grow

Be honest that you don't possess all of the skills necessary for the new position. In truth, there will be very few candidates who are perfectly qualified. If they are still speaking with you, they have noticed something in you that will benefit their business. You must have a plan in place to upskill yourself further, whether this is registering online with another training facility, university, or college. Maybe it's being able to find an after-hours tutor or a mentor. Being able to indicate to the client that you are prepared to do whatever it takes to upskill yourself as quickly as possible will confirm that you are the right candidate for the job.

Be Flexible

One of the biggest benefits of being a mid-career shifter rather than someone fresh out of college is that you have years' worth of experience behind you. With this experience comes the ability to be flexible and adapt with changes within the work environment. This skill sometimes takes years to develop, and those who are years behind you have not had the work experience to guarantee that they are able to contribute in a positive way.

Highlight Advantages in Your Past Career

Although you may have indicated this on your career resume already, be prepared to highlight advantages in your previous career that can possibly be utilized across both careers. Provide examples of where you have had to make use of these skills to resolve problems in the workplace, or to add value.

Be Aware of Cultural Shifts

Each organization has its own business culture and guaranteed, where you are coming from is not going to be anything like where you are going. Sure, there are bound to be some similarities, but there are also likely to be more cultural differences. Be prepared to face up to these and embrace them. Provide the hiring manager with examples of where you've had to be a team player, or part of a multicultural team, and how this was approached.

The Art of Negotiation

So, the interview process has gone better than expected and the recruiter/hiring manager is at the point of extending an offer. Assuming that you have gotten this far, and the recruitment process has been followed to the letter, an extensive and exhaustive recruitment procedure has been followed. Possibly hundreds of resumes were scanned sorting through candidates who met the minimum criteria for the job. Next came the initial screening process, followed by a round of assessments and interviews. Depending on the exact procedure used, additional assessments have been completed and you've probably been invited back for a second round of interviews, or a panel interview. Now comes the time for the offer to be extended. For many organizations this happens through the individual who has conducted most of the interviews, or the Human Resources (HR) department. This process changes from one organization to the next but is usually done formally in writing. The written offer will normally outline all benefits attached to the package that the company is prepared to offer you. This is where the negotiation process begins.

A formal offer in writing doesn't need to be accepted on the spot, and there's ALWAYS room for negotiation. Depending on the job opening you've applied for, the company is always open to negotiation. It's an expected norm for negotiation to take place. The following are some key points regarding negotiation:

- Never sign the offer immediately—take some time to think it over, even if it's just 24 hours.

- Never assume that the offer on the table is the best offer available. It never is and there's almost always money still on the table.

- If you are applying for a position where you are working with people, sales, manipulation, or negotiation, your offer may be your first test with the organization to see whether or not you are going to negotiate with them. Chances are, if you don't, the hiring manager is going to be questioning whether they've made the right call or not.

There's an expression that if you don't ask, you don't get. Sometimes you need to pluck up the courage and ask for what it is that you want. What's the worst that can happen? You can be told "no." What would you have lost during the process? Absolutely nothing! Whereas, if you ask for another 500 to 1,000 dollars per month, it could add up to a substantial amount of money.

In some instances. it's not about the financial numbers. There are plenty of other things you could be negotiating with, like signing bonuses, relocation packages, travel allowances, or even covering the costs of your mobile phone. Companies are often prepared to pay for tuition, which is something you may need in order to conform to industry standards. There are many things that you can negotiate on. The major takeaway from this section is there's always something more that you can negotiate with the company for, and you don't need to settle for the first number put on paper in front of you.

Don't stack yourself up against others in the industry, questioning whether you can perform the duties as well as the next person. This will drive you crazy, but also, if the company or organization wanted to go that route, they would have made an offer to a candidate with that background. Remember that your work experience (even in another industry) counts for something, and you may not need to start all over again with as big a gap as you thought.

In every job opening there's a salary scale that's either advertised or discussed during the interview process. Before you begin applying for positions, you should have already calculated what your bare minimum salary expectation would be. If the offer is nowhere near there, and there's no possible way to reach that goal, you need to know what the number is when you walk away. Too often people accept jobs out of sheer desperation, and although the offer is much lower than they actually needed, they believe that it's the only chance they're likely to get—especially when switching careers.

What if it's not the only chance? What if the perfect job is waiting for you, just around the corner? Don't be too quick to sign on the dotted line before the ink on the proposal is even dry. Take a day or so to work through the proposed offer before either accepting it or rejecting it. Chances are that the new figures may be exactly what you're looking for. Shifting careers does not mean having to start at an entry level position again.

Do your best to connect directly with the hiring manager rather than human resources or a recruiter. The hiring manager has the power (and possibly the budget) to make things happen and to negotiate. They know what their staffing budget is for the year and are fully aware of any wiggle room that may be had. Chances are that you're replacing someone who had been with the company for a while and so their salary would not be an entry level one. If you have done your homework through PayScale or Glassdoor, you already have the salary scales for these positions.

Negotiate a possible salary review within your first three to six months. This could be on the basis of meeting company objectives or other strategic plans that the organization may want to put in place, similar to milestones. This will indicate that you're willing to prove your worth to the organization and its business goals.

During your salary negotiation process with the hiring manager, be confident and anticipate that the meeting is going to be a positive one. Show them the respect they deserve, without coming across as arrogant or demanding. This could sour a working relationship before it has even begun.

Having completed all your financial calculations right at the beginning of this process, you will already be aware of what your family needs to survive. If the offers on the table are lower than this, there's no point in pursuing the interview process further and you must be prepared to walk away. While no hiring manager wants to hear that they need to begin the recruitment process all over again, rather now than in two months' time when you're desperately scrambling to find enough money to pay the rent or put food on the table. You must be realistic in your approach and remember that it's just business. Your home and family life needs to be balanced and come before your work. Although work essentially supports the home and family, you cannot maintain balance if your salary is so far out. It will just frustrate you, and you'll end up punishing yourself for walking away from a brilliant career where you were all safe and secure!

Keys to Success on Your Journey

Turning Fear on its Head

Fear of the unknown is probably one of the biggest challenges you will need to face during this transition period. It's natural to experience some anxiety over what the future holds. At any given time, changing careers has been proven to be one of the most stressful experiences that anyone can go through. Doing a complete switch mid-career is more than scary for anyone. This is why most people remain stuck in their dead-end jobs, miserable and dissatisfied. It all comes down to one single four-letter word—fear!

What if you could get fear under control? It's entirely possible by altering the way you approach the fear and adding a question to it. Find another folio pad, or the same one that you've been working in all along. Pick a quiet time or set aside time when you know you're least likely to be disturbed. Identify all those things that you are currently afraid of. Chances are this list will include things like:

- Can I afford to pay for my home, my car, my kids tuition, and all other living expenses?
- What if I fail?
- What if I make a complete fool out of myself?
- What if changing careers is a mistake?

You may have other items on your list, but this will give you a basic idea of some of the nagging thoughts that could begin to weigh you down. Fear can actually be a good thing because it means that you are considering things logically and you're not living in a rose-tinted bubble where everything is just perfect. You can work through each of your fears by turning them into "how" questions. Examples of this would be:

- How am I going to afford all my monthly living expenses?
- How can I fail?
- How am I likely to make a fool out of myself?
- How can changing careers be a mistake?

Notice that they already seem more manageable and your brain is starting to look for solutions, rather than merely seeing problems? Fear can motivate us to move beyond doubt and into a space where we can make our dreams a reality, rather than automatically assuming something before you've given it a chance to work. By adding the word "how" to the question, you can act in such a way that you break each fear down into an actionable stepping stone.

Don't Look for Perfection

Most candidates move to other jobs because they are unhappy. It's very seldom about the money; often it's based on other people, being unhappy with their environment, or no longer feeling satisfied with what they are doing. Almost everyone who looks to make a midlife career shift is at the point where they're questioning whether their life has meaning or not. They are beginning to question whether what they are doing is having a positive impact on society. They are actually seeking perfection from a job, and the reality is that there is no perfect job out there. Various jobs have "perfect" aspects to them. As a whole, you will always be chasing a pipedream when looking for the one perfect job. If this is what you're after, reality will eventually set in, and you will discover that even the new position has certain elements that are far from perfect.

Be realistic towards your new work and accept there will be days that won't always be perfect. It will broaden your perspective and prevent you from expecting something that's never going to happen.

Be Persistent

When it comes to achieving goals, remember to use the SMART goal setting method. Be persistent and confident in everything you do as you change careers. Break each of your goals down into smaller manageable chunks, so that you begin to achieve them one at a time. There's no point to setting massive, unrealistic goals, especially when first starting out. Set smaller daily goals and begin to move from there. Never lose sight of what you're trying to achieve overall, but don't try to do it all at once.

Step by Step

Approach everything one step at a time, especially during your transition phase. Trying to do too much all at once can overwhelm you and make it easier to give up any long-term plans. Remember that you need to break things down. You cannot immediately become a master at something unless you've first been the apprentice. Any athlete begins training slowly and systematically. There must be a warm-up session, then some basic training that helps strengthen muscles. Only much later does one begin with endurance and learning how to go the distance. It all begins with a single step though.

Persevere

Throwing the towel in, especially after a minor defeat or the first obstacle that comes your way, should not be an option. Learning to persevere is a skill that will prove useful throughout your life. It's easy to give up and walk away every time we experience a situation we don't like or that makes us uncomfortable. We need to learn to move past petty issues and rise above them. Perseverance is also applicable when it comes to achieving our goals. We cannot give up each time we encounter a roadblock or barrier in front of us.

Take a Break

During a transition period, we are normally so busy focusing our efforts and attention on getting things done to switch careers that we often neglect ourselves. We need to be mindful of this and ensure that we take regular breaks. Our bodies need time to rest and rejuvenate, and the only way to do this is by relaxing. We cannot be on the go permanently without experiencing some form of burnout. Allow yourself regular time to do things that you enjoy, things that will take your mind off of all the busyness of a career transition. Allow yourself to do things that you enjoy. Learn to unplug, get out in nature, share special moments with friends and family. Most of all, get your mind off all things related to your career.

Set Your Own Goals for Success

The world measures success on the basis of fame, fortune, the fancy home, how many cars you have, and an entire gamut of other things. You know what is going to make you happy and what is going to bring your family happiness. It's these things that should motivate you to try to achieve greater things. Don't work to prove something to individuals who have no influence over your life. You should be working to support your loved ones and your family. They are the individuals that matter, and more importantly, you should be doing this for you. Identify those things that will make you happy. That's the goal that you should be striving for.

Believe

One of the most powerful words is 'believe.' Believe in your own abilities and that you alone have the power to make your dreams and goals a reality. You were destined for great things, and only you can make it happen. While believing is good, it needs to be followed up with action. If you combine the two, you are certain to experience success. Remember to give yourself time once you switch careers. You need to be able to settle in and learn the ropes correctly. Don't be excessively hard on yourself and/or unrealistic, even if transitioning into your new career takes longer than expected. Sometimes slower transitions, or a gradual approach can work out just as well.

Conclusion

"You have to be burning with an idea, or a problem, or a wrong that you want to right. If you're not passionate enough from the start, you'll never stick it out."

~ Steve Jobs

Accept that any major change you make to your life is one of the most challenging and difficult things you'll ever have to face. There's also no guarantee that it's going to be a success. There are some important lessons to be learned from those that have gone before and actually managed to be part of that 50% we discussed right at the beginning of this book. According to Joseph Liu, professional business coach who has worked helping others all over the world, there are a couple of commonalities to be found with those who have been successful. Having interviewed 50 of these individuals, this is what he came up with (Liu, 2019).

Get Ready for Upheaval

Change is disruptive and scary no matter the size of the move. You should accept that your life is never going to be the same, ever again.

Update Your Network

Networking can make all the difference between success or failure in your new venture. Don't expect results or support from your old network. We become like the people we associate with most often. If you're planning on walking away from a long-term career, be careful who you share this information with. There will always be the naysayers and prophets of doom and gloom telling you to stay where you are. Your sanity is your own and you need to protect it from the negativity of these individuals at all costs. Look for a whole new group of positive individuals.

Change Takes Time

There are no shortcuts to achieving success or stepping out of your comfort zone to begin something new. If there were, and if this was something that was comfortable, everyone would be doing it. Instead, be prepared for your new career to take time and be realistic with yourself. There are very few instances of anything becoming an overnight success. It all takes time and dedicated effort to become successful.

Daily Deliberate Actions

Set your sights on choosing to perform daily deliberate actions that are going to move your career in the right direction. A shift in trajectory is one thing, but it's not going to happen automatically. You need to focus on the small things each and every day, and you'd be amazed how quickly the big things begin to take care of themselves.

Knowing When to Walk Away

Having all the tools and insights into shifting careers is great, but if it's not working, there's no point in bashing your head against a brick wall. If your new career is not working out the way you thought it would, at some stage you need to be prepared to walk away. This may mean looking for another alternative, or in some instances returning to what you know. If this happens, please don't see it as failure; see it as another opportunity for you to reinvent yourself.

Your Journey is Unique

Every career shift experience is as different and unique as the individual going through the journey. Don't compare your experiences with those of the next person, because they're not. Your success or failure hinges on you and can have a multitude of other factors influencing the trajectory that your career takes. Allow the process to unfold naturally, putting your best effort in, but enjoy the journey while it lasts. Record the highs and lows of your experiences so you can someday share them as part of your story.

Become Excited

Your new career is an exciting journey and should be one that you get to explore entirely. Exploring requires an inquisitive mind, open to learning new ideas and gaining new experience. Allow yourself to be open to this and anticipate some steep learning curves. While immersing yourself entirely in your new career, allow yourself to experience new things without any anticipation. This is similar to being mindful. Allow yourself to experience each new part of your career, but don't hold onto any of your new experiences too tightly. Slowly allow them to become part of who you are—the new you.

When Energy Trumps Passion

It's one thing trying to find and follow your passion, while on the other hand, you should really be searching for increased energy. This is what is going to get you out of bed in the morning. It's what's going to keep you excited and motivated throughout the day. Passion can fade, so strive instead for that which excites you, energizes you, and restores your soul.

What's Your New Story?

This often bothers a lot of individuals who have successfully transitioned into their new career or are still in the process. You become so bent on having one specific label that has defined you and your career up to this point. How do you now categorize yourself? How do you explain your new career to others when they ask? It's important to be aware of the story you are going to create to explain to others what you're currently doing. You are ideally looking for those around you to provide you with support, rather than sitting in judgement. This may necessitate reducing your circle of friends and support group if they are more cynical than supportive.

Slow and Steady

The kiddies narrative of the tortoise and the hare is a perfect example of this. Allow yourself time to settle in your newfound career. Don't expect to be perfect at it from the very first day. Give yourself time to learn new things and gain new skills that will benefit you in eventually gaining all the skills necessary to perform your new career at your peak.

Trust Your Gut

As humans, there's one gift that we all possess: an inner voice, or that feeling you get deep in your gut. Trust it because it's seldom wrong. Even if you've just made a career change and you're suddenly beginning to feel uneasy about it, question why. Do your best to get to the bottom of it. You may have made a mistake or been too hasty in trying to make the switch, or you may just be so used to your previous job security that this is all something new to you. Whatever is weighing you down, try to identify the real reason for feeling as you do.

We've managed to cover a lot of ground when it comes to being able to analyze where you are in your career right now and discovering the thing(s) that motivate you the most.

You've done a deep dive into your strengths and weaknesses, as well as completed extensive research on careers that are out there that may be a potential match; you are aware of those skills you can transfer to any new position and may even have a few good ideas of careers you could be considering. Most of the work has been deeply introspective and you've had to look inwards a lot, rather than outwards.

Using the information provided, you should have been able to discover your Ikigai, which should have helped you with identifying your life work or your true purpose.

Being specific on what you want from a career, as well as from life, can help you achieve your true purpose.

Understanding financial obligations and pressure that may well accompany your decision is probably one of your biggest considerations. Financial stability is necessary even if you claim that it's not important. Remember that you still need to be able to live, and the only way to do that is with money.

Exploring career options can be fun. Look at including some volunteer work, or job shadowing, or interview/speak to other professionals in the industry to see if they can give you pointers. Be realistic and consider that you may need to take a substantial pay-cut to get to what you currently 'think' you want.

Do as much as you can to learn new skills that can be used in your new career. This can often be done while you're still comfortably employed. This will act as a safety net.

It's never advisable to simply throw the towel in on a whim. Get everything sorted out and ready before you even consider handing in your resignation. You may get involved with studying towards your new career and discover that there are a whole lot of things you never knew about the career and it's not such a great fit after all.

The most important takeaways are:
- You don't need to be stuck in a job you hate just because you're rapidly heading towards

the midway point of your career. You are never too old to change careers, as long as all the work has been done prior to simply jumping ship. Don't leave your career change too late, but make certain that it's what you really want to be doing.

- You deserve to be happy in a job that you love—there are so many opportunities available out there, you just need to know where to look and take the risk when you find the right one.

- Everything in life is a negotiation. When it comes to signing on the dotted line, remember that they specifically want you. Don't be too afraid or insecure in your own skin to ask for what you deserve. Know your real worth.

- Finally, making a change today, doesn't mean you have to stick with it forever! If you discover you've made a terrible mistake, simply fix it and learn to move on.

Now that you know How to Find a Job You Love and you have all the tools at your disposal, get on out there and make them work for you!

If you enjoyed the book, please leave a review on Amazon.

References

Biography.com Editors. (2017, April 28). *Henry Ford Biography*. Biography. https://www.biography.com/business-figure/henry-ford

Brazen. (2013, May 16). *10 tips for changing careers without losing your mind*. Brazen. https://www.brazen.com/resources/10-tips-for-changing-careers-without-losing-your-mind

Buettner, D. (2012). *The Blue Zones : 9 lessons for living longer from the people who've lived the longest*. National Geographic.

Burry, M. (2019, November 27). *7 Things you can do to make your next job change successful*. The Balance Careers. https://www.thebalancecareers.com/how-to-make-your-next-job-change-a-success-4582744

Burry, M. (2020a, January 8). *Tips on how to ace your interview if you are switching careers*. The Balance Careers. https://www.thebalancecareers.com/tips-for-career-change-interviews-4144981

Burry, M. (2020b, May 21). *Tips on writing a powerful career change resume*. The Balance Careers. https://www.thebalancecareers.com/career-change-resume-writing-tips-4134292

Caprino, K. (2012a, January 2). *5 Core steps to a more satisfying career in 2012*. Forbes. https://www.forbes.com/sites/kathycaprino/2012/01/02/5-core-steps-to-a-more-satisfying-career-in-2012/

Caprino, K. (2012b, January 26). *The 8 stages of career transformation*. Forbes. https://www.forbes.com/sites/kathycaprino/2012/01/26/the-8-stages-of-career-transformation/

Caprino, K. (2013a, June 20). *5 ways to tell if you need a career change*. Forbes. https://www.forbes.com/sites/kathycaprino/2013/06/20/5-ways-to-tell-if-you-need-a-career-change/

Caprino, K. (2013b, July 19). *What NOT to do when leaving your job*. HuffPost. https://www.huffpost.com/entry/5-biggest-mistakes-career-changers-make_b_3581148

Conlan, C. (n.d.). *10 awesome free career self-assessment tools on the Internet*. Monster Career Advice. https://www.monster.com/career-advice/article/best-free-career-assessment-tools

Covey, S. R. (2013). *7 Habits of highly effective people*. Simon & Schuster Ltd. (Original work published 1990)

Delaney, P. (2019, July 15). *How to write a career change cover letter [+example]*. Resume

Genius. https://resumegenius.com/blog/cover-letter-help/career-change-cover-letter

Doyle, A. (2019, May 9). *Sample career change cover letter and writing tips*. The Balance Careers. https://www.thebalancecareers.com/sample-career-change-cover-letter-2060185

Elizaga, K. (2014). *Find your sweet spot : a guide to personal and professional excellence*. Skirt!, An Imprint Of Globe Pequot Press.

Evans, L. (2014, February 5). *How to navigate the tricky waters of a career change*. Fast Company. https://www.fastcompany.com/3026011/how-to-navigate-the-tricky-waters-of-a-career-change

Graham, D. (2018, June 29). *How to Negotiate for a Better Salary When You're Switching Careers*. Medium. https://medium.com/s/story/how-to-negotiate-for-a-better-salary-when-youres-switching-careers-8a36bae307c9

Hamm, T. (2008, April 6). *Ten killer tactics for developing a new skill*. The Simple Dollar. https://www.thesimpledollar.com/financial-wellness/ten-killer-tactics-for-developing-a-new-skill/

Helmuth, L. (2015, August 5). *5 Tips for changing careers*. Blog.Dce.Harvard.Edu.

https://blog.dce.harvard.edu/extension/5-tips-changing-careers

Henry, A. (2013, October 6). *What should I know before I change careers?* Lifehacker. https://www.lifehacker.com/what-should-i-know-before-i-change-careers-512289050

Howington, J. (2015, March 25). *5 Career change obstacles you may confront.* FlexJobs Job Search Tips and Blog. https://www.flexjobs.com/blog/post/5-career-change-obstacles-may-confront/

Indeed Career Development. (2019). *How to develop your skill set to advance your career | Indeed.com.* Indeed.Com. https://www.indeed.com/career-advice/career-development/how-to-develop-your-skill-set

Joblist Blog. (2019, November 5). *Midlife career crisis | Joblist.* Www.Joblist.Com. https://www.joblist.com/trends/midlife-career-crisis

Liu, J. (2019, April 2). *How to change careers, according to 50 people who made A pivot.* Forbes. https://www.forbes.com/sites/josephliu/2019/04/02/successfully-change-careers/

Lowe, A. (2010, November 9). *The 50 best work and passion quotes of all time.* The One-Week Job Project. https://www.oneweekjob.com/blog/blog/20

10/11/09/the-50-best-work-and-passion-quotes-of-all-time

Mitsuhashi, Y. (2017, August 7). *Ikigai: A Japanese concept to improve work and life.* Www.Bbc.Com. https://www.bbc.com/worklife/article/20170807-ikigai-a-japanese-concept-to-improve-work-and-life

People at Heart Coaching. (n.d.). *Finding your Ikigai | 8 questions to explore the reason that gets you out of bed.* Career Coaching in London | People at Heart | Find a Career That Makes You Happy. https://www.peopleatheartcoaching.com/finding-your-ikigai

Profita, M. (2020, February 12). *10 steps to successfully changing your career.* The Balance Careers. https://www.thebalancecareers.com/successful-career-change-2058452

Stanley, N. (n.d.). *How to network your way into a new career (without feeling like a slimy, lying con artist) | Careershifters.* Www.Careershifters.Org. https://www.careershifters.org/expert-advice/how-to-network-your-way-into-a-new-career

Suzuki, A., & Central Research Services Inc. (n.d.). *Public opinion survey on "ikigai."* Www.Crs.or.Jp.

https://www.crs.or.jp/backno/No636/6362.htm

Sweatt, L. (2018, July 31). *19 Quotes about following your passion*. SUCCESS. https://www.success.com/19-quotes-about-following-your-passion/

The Balance Careers. (2011). *Free career aptitude and career assessment tests*. The Balance Careers. https://www.thebalancecareers.com/free-career-aptitude-tests-2059813

The Undercover Recruiter. (2015, January 28). *10 Career-change questions to ask yourself before jumping ship*. Undercover Recruiter. https://theundercoverrecruiter.com/career-change-questions-to-ask-yourself/

Thetford, C. (n.d.). *What to say in a career change interview*. The Muse. https://www.themuse.com/advice/4-smart-ways-to-spin-a-career-change-in-your-favor-during-an-interview

Torres, B. (2014, April). *50 Inspirational career quotes*. Themuse.Com; The Muse. https://www.themuse.com/advice/50-inspirational-career-quotes

Warley, S. (2016, March 17). *Find your why to get unstuck*. Life Skills That Matter. https://lifeskillsthatmatter.com/find-your-why/

Westlake, J. (n.d.). *5 Steps to writing a cover letter as a career changer (with samples!)*. Themuse.Com. https://www.themuse.com/advice/career-change-cover-letter-sample

Yate, M. (2018, February 9). *The 7 transferable skills to help you change careers*. Forbes. https://www.forbes.com/sites/nextavenue/2018/02/09/the-7-transferable-skills-to-help-you-change-careers/#3197f19e4c04

Image References

athree23 from Pixabay. (n.d.). Marketing concept idea. In *Pixabay.com*. https://pixabay.com/photos/whiteboard-marketing-idea-concept-4876651/

Content Pixie from Pexels. (n.d.). Ikigai book candles stones. In *Pexels.com*. https://www.pexels.com/photo/photo-of-candles-stones-and-book-2736542/

Ekrulila from Pexels. (n.d.). Person holding white scroll. In *Pexels.com*. https://www.pexels.com/photo/person-holding-white-scroll-2292837/

Franz Roos from Pixabay. (n.d.). Overwhelmed stressed out. In *Pixabay.com*. https://pixabay.com/photos/overwhelmed-stressed-out-burned-out-4592797/

Gerd Altmann from Pixabay. (n.d.). Job offer hiring sign. In *Pixabay.com*. https://pixabay.com/photos/job-job-offer-workplace-job-search-2860035/

Lukas Bieri from Pixabay. (n.d.). Blogger screenwriter. In *Pixabay.com*. https://pixabay.com/photos/youtuber-blogger-screenwriter-2838945/

StockSnap at Pixabay. (n.d.). Woman on mountain. In *Pixabay.com*. https://pixabay.com/photos/people-woman-travel-adventure-trek-2591874/

Sue Styles from Pixabay. (n.d.). Interview women. In *Pixabay.com*. https://pixabay.com/photos/interview-deal-business-handshake-4835116/

Ylanite Koppens from Pixabay. (n.d.-a). Book still life make it happen. In *Pixabay.com*. https://pixabay.com/photos/still-life-paper-no-person-3126536/

Ylanite Koppens from Pixabay. (n.d.-b). Work space life plan. In *Pixabay.com*. https://pixabay.com/photos/flatlay-work-workspace-office-3938877/

Your Unlimited Opportunities & the Art of Personal Transformation

How to teach yourself anything, control your fate and make life easier now

Clement Harrison

Introduction

When you feel unable to get ahead in life, this can put you in a tough place. Feelings of doubt will take over your mind, convincing you that your dreams and aspirations are unattainable. This can cause you to feel isolated and misunderstood, especially when you want to improve yourself, but you don't know how. With the help of this book, you will discover a pathway to follow during the moments when you are unsure of what to do next. Through working on these strategies and tips, you will be able to become the best version of yourself and outperform many people who are trying to do the same thing with a different approach.

As you read on, you will discover many methods that you can apply to your life instantly. This process does not have to be delayed any longer because you have what it takes right now to harness your energy and put it to good use. What you thought was impossible before will seem easier when you become a more balanced, motivated, healthier, smarter, and more purposeful person. By being able to process information, you will understand how to concentrate and focus with ease, successfully finding solutions for the problems that plague you.

My name is Clement Harrison, and I am a Neuroeconomics expert. After taking up an interest in self-improvement, I decided to embrace a path as a personal development coach as well. I have taught many people about the ins and outs of personal motivation, neuroscience, and economics. It feels great to know that I can teach people a wide variety of subjects, but what really drives me is the satisfaction that I get in knowing that my teachings are helping people on a daily basis. When they apply my teachings to their everyday lives, they become more successful.

It is my firm belief that your wealth depends upon the good you do in your life. Because of this, I have been inspired to pursue my passion. I founded my own management consulting firm that specializes in helping people. No matter who you are or what walk of life you are currently in, the goal is to enrich your life by helping you to become the best version you can be. You do not need to offer other people a lot to offer them something valuable. It is amazing what taking the time to be carefully considerate can do for someone's self-esteem.

After you read this book, you will have all of the knowledge you need to take matters into your own hands. Not only will you feel empowered at the moment, but you will be capable of determining what you must do to make better choices. The key is to stop worrying about what others think of you. There are always going to be onlookers, and they might offer their opinions, but that does not mean you have to take their advice or listen to their criticism. With the confidence that you will have after reading these methods, you will understand how to concentrate effortlessly. After learning these new skills, you will be able to concentrate on anything that life throws your way. Life can be incredibly unpredictable, but this does not have to be a negative thing.

People continuously thank me for how these methods have positively impacted their lives and changed them for the better. Many expressed how they never imagined they would be able to feel so confident or special, and this brings me a lot of joy as a personal development coach. Because so many people constantly express their thanks, it further proves that these methods are easy for anyone to follow. Broken down into easy to understand steps, it does not have to be hard to transform your life. You are going to see real results that will last.

With my help and knowledge, you are going to thrive in today's world. These steps are actionable, meaning you will get the results that you crave. After seeing how much progress you are able to make in the beginning, this is going to propel you forward and keep you motivated for the future. Those dreams you have on hold will be reignited as you work on ways to pursue them once again. With a mindset that is completely transformed and reshaped, you will surely be able to outperform your competition.

Making any kind of life change is scary, but what happens if you keep doing the same thing? You are going to experience the same results. Nothing is going to change if you continue with the same patterns and habits that you have always kept. You should start to work on being the best version of yourself you can be now instead of prolonging your disappointment. The more you grow as a person, the more opportunities you will have access to. You will be glad that you took the leap and started changing your behaviors.

You only have this life to live, so you should make the most of it. Would you rather continue on being unhappy and unfulfilled? Know that you have a choice, and you can change the way you feel by changing your outlook on life. If you are ready to take meaningful action now, you are going to gain so many beneficial skills that you can use for the rest of your life. You will see how easily accessible most of these skills are, and you will wonder why you haven't gotten started sooner. You deserve to live the life you dream of, filled with success and happiness.

Chapter 1: Why Improving Yourself Matters

From an early age, we are taught that education is important. For most children, getting a formal education and being expected to succeed is the foundation of childhood. After schooling has been completed, we are expected to get a job that allows us to support ourselves and be successful. This constant desire to be better and to do better can come with a lot of pressure, especially when you are struggling. Life doesn't always work out exactly as planned, especially when it comes to your education and career. This doesn't mean that all hope is lost for improvement. In fact, self-improvement is more important than ever when you are struggling in life.

Its importance often goes unnoticed, but self-improvement is a driving force in your life, even right now. Whether you tend to brush your shortcomings aside in an effort to get over them, or you set your focus on them to the point where it drives you crazy. There must be a balance for you to feel good about the life you are living. When you pay attention to self-improvement, you are committing to having more self-awareness. This means you are able to take responsibility for your actions. You will have a better understanding of what you do and why. This is important because it can offer you insight into what you should do next.

As you begin working on improving yourself, you will learn how to identify your strengths. Once you know what you are working with, you will better understand how you can use them to your advantage. For example, I had to show myself what I was capable of. Through this learning process, I discovered that I am a great peacemaker, always trying to step in when my loved ones were arguing. This is a great strength that helps me work through problems that affect other people as well as myself. I learned how to use it during times of conflict to help reduce stress. It wasn't always this clear to me, though. I spent many years wondering if I was good at anything at all.

Another side of self-improvement comes from recognizing your weaknesses—everyone has them. You don't need to allow them to hold you back, however. By identifying what they are, you will know what you need to work on, even what you can do to turn them into strengths. Having weaknesses is nothing to be ashamed of, as that will only hold you back further. All of the traits you possess are a part of your personality. As you work on improving yourself, you should make it an effort to look beyond any weaknesses you have right now and realize that you can work on them. While it might not be easy to do, it isn't impossible.

Your comfort zone is exactly how it sounds—comfortable. This can be a secure place to be in life, but it is not a place that will lead you to improvement. Getting out of your comfort zone is one of the most essential parts of truly improving yourself. While it might feel scary to do this, especially when you don't have many outside factors telling you that it should be done, it is something you should push yourself to do anyway. This is how you will grow. Getting out of your comfort zone forces you to be strategic. You must think differently to gain all of the resources that you need to live a happy life. This change will allow you to broaden your way of thinking, encouraging you to step outside of your comfort zone in the future continually.

One of the biggest reasons you should make it a priority to work on improving yourself is because this will improve your mental health, as well. If you have been struggling and feeling like you are in a rut in life lately, your mental health has probably declined. This is not only upsetting, but it can be dangerous. You need to take care of yourself, both physically and mentally. By placing a priority on your mental health, you will realize that self-improvement is for the better. It is meant to help you cope with your feelings and work on problem-solving techniques. Nothing that life throws your way will debilitate you any longer. With the skills you learn from reading this book, you will learn how to be even more resilient than you already are.

How Your Past Shapes Your Life

Your past is partially responsible for the person you are today. The experiences you've been through have shaped you and molded your personality. While your past does not determine exactly how your life is going to unfold in the future, it does hold some weight over your traits and characteristics. If you have been through trauma or other unfortunate circumstances, this might make you a naturally guarded person. While this is only one example of the way your past can shape your present, it happens more commonly than you would think. Even if you have experienced hardship that you believe you are over today, those memories still subconsciously impact you.

In some cases, your past can cause a lot of damage to your life. If you are unable to let go of the things that happened to you, this can lead to needless suffering. It is hard just to turn your brain off, especially after something has already happened. You might replay the incident over and over until you can no longer feel the pain or suffering. This numbness is only temporary, though. The cycle continues to repeat itself as long as you let it.

Some examples of self-limiting beliefs include:

"I'm too old."

"I don't know enough about this."

"Someone else can do this better than me."

While these are all valid statements about how you might feel, you need to realize that only you are stopping yourself if you bring up these points. There are plenty of other ways that you stop yourself from doing things because of similar reasons. It is important to recognize them so you can curb this behavior. Getting into a habit of relying on excuses will only leave you feeling discouraged and disappointed.

These beliefs are formed early in life, often beginning in childhood. Depending on your upbringing, your self-confidence starts to develop when you are very young. If you received constant encouragement from your guardian(s), your self-esteem likely thrived because you were shown support. If you weren't so lucky, this might have led you to the issues that you face today. The way you were raised is not your fault. Even if you had a terrible childhood that instilled many fears and bad views about yourself, know that it isn't on you to take the blame.

The brain naturally picks up on patterns, even as children. If your guardian(s) set these examples for you, it is only natural that you would pick them up and make them a regular part of your life. As an adult, these patterns become more apparent if you look for them. It can be an upsetting discovery, but the good news is that you can now identify them. From there, change is possible. While your core beliefs are strong and deeply rooted, you can change the way that you act on them to help you live a happier and healthier life.

Self-limiting behavior does not stop at your personal life. It can also make its way into your professional life. In the workplace, you might feel inadequate due to your childhood upbringing. This might prevent you from going for opportunities that you feel you are not qualified to handle. What you need to overcome is the power of positive thinking. You have a lot of power when you learn how to shape your thoughts more positively and productively.

When you put some effort into thinking positively, you will see how much your current circumstances change. While some things might feel like they are set in stone, this is never the case—your life is ever-changing, and you can use this as a source of comfort. Instead of getting caught up in negativity, it makes a lot more sense to put a positive spin on whatever is going on in your life. This will motivate you to rise above the situation, looking for solutions wherever you go.

By thinking positively, you will also bring a new purpose into your life. Everything you do will make sense and have a point. Many people end up feeling discouraged when they realize that they do not think they have a purpose in life. This can, understandably, cause someone to give up on their goals and dreams if they cannot see anything worthwhile in their future. By always giving yourself something to strive for, you will always have something to look forward to. This is positive enough in itself, but it can further harness your positive thoughts to motivate you along the way as well.

Letting Go

Once you know what your self-limiting behaviors are, you can make a plan to change them. Free yourself from their confines, and know that you are capable of letting go of your past. As you navigate through your feelings, you'll notice two specific types of beliefs that have formed over time: destination beliefs and directive beliefs. The former are conclusions, while the latter are signs that guide you toward your destination. For example, you might have a destination belief that you do not fit in with other groups of people. This conclusion might have developed due to past experiences in your life, but now you continue to reinforce it.

Your directive beliefs will tell you that you are bothering people when you walk in the room, or that you should just keep your mouth shut when thinking about speaking up about what matters to you. Overall, if you have a lonely and outcast destination set for yourself, the rest of your behaviors will lead you to a self-fulfilling prophecy. These feelings are so hard to overcome because they prey on your subconscious mind. This is why you might have to work at changing them for a long time before you see any results. It is difficult to change what you cannot immediately see, but that does not mean it is impossible.

By getting your conscious mind aligned with your unconscious mind, you will be able to spot your self-sabotage moments. Using the above example, imagine that you were invited to a work function that is being thrown for all staff members. Because you feel like an outcast, you decline the invitation while using the excuse that you won't go because no one there likes you. Your insecurities might be sending you this exact message, but what factual information can you use to back this up? Have any of your peers ever directly told you that you aren't welcome at the function or that they do not like you? These are important issues to address to get to the bottom of your unconscious thoughts.

To overcome your limiting beliefs, you must take back control over them. The things that you have been resisting most are the things that you most need to let go of. In this case, it would be your lingering conclusion that everyone dislikes you. Your limiting beliefs play off of your fears, so this is why they can feel so real. A lot of people fear failure, so your limiting beliefs will do everything they can to convince you that you are failing in some way. It helps to realize how much control you have over your conscious thoughts and how much this can help shape your unconscious ones.

There are three steps you can take when you feel that your self-limiting behavior is getting in the way of living your best life:

1. When your day begins, acknowledge that there will always be a part of you that craves familiarity. If this happens to be negative thought patterns and self-sabotaging tendencies, your mind is going to have a hard pull toward these thoughts and behaviors. Accept this about yourself because it is natural to feel this way.

2. Tell yourself that you will pay close attention to your directive beliefs. These signs that you spot that seemingly tell you what to do aren't always right. If your directive beliefs are making you miserable, this can be a sign to look within. Ask yourself what you truly believe and identify why these beliefs can be so difficult to manage.

3. No matter what directive belief comes your way, acknowledge it, and challenge it if you need to. Anything that makes you feel negative should be challenged. Ask yourself if this belief is valid, and give yourself the proof to back it up. If you cannot find adequate proof, this is likely a sign that your negative thoughts created the belief.

This isn't a fool-proof plan to make you let go of your past woes and think positively from this moment on, but it is a way to get started. Everyone must start somewhere, and taking the initiative is what is necessary. Understand that you cannot shift all of your thoughts to conscious ones, but you can better interpret what you need in life by paying attention to your unconscious ones. The more that you work on thinking positively, the more you will notice your directives change. They will begin to look more promising, no longer focusing on the daunting "what-ifs" that life tends to bring your way.

Understand that you got to an unhappy place in your life because of your unconscious. You did not wake up one day and decide that you wanted to be unhappy. This showcases how powerful your thoughts are as a whole. Forgive yourself for reaching this point, understanding that it became comfortable and easy to settle into a place like this. Your time to change is now, though. By working on ways to let go and move forward, you will start to see little glimmers of happiness everywhere you turn.

Change the Way You See Yourself

Starting any change from within is the easiest way to go about it. While you might not be able to control many external factors that impact your life, there is always a chance for you to transform yourself for the better. If you are ready to transition into your positive way of thinking, work on incorporating these tips into your life:

- **Be True to Your Word**: Your word is one of the strongest promises you can make. If you make a commitment to something or someone, always keep this to uphold your integrity. As you prove to yourself, and those around you, that you can follow through, this is going to make you feel better about yourself. When you realize that it doesn't take much effort to be a dependable person, you will likely have few problems holding yourself accountable for your commitments.

    When you break promises, you aren't only letting those around you down. You are also letting yourself down. Even if these broken promises do not directly impact you, you are still going to feel their effects. It isn't a great feeling to know that you didn't follow through because this equates to failure. Instead of putting yourself into situations where you are automatically going to fail, you can make it a point to become better about keeping your promises and staying true to your word.

- **Don't Take Things Personally**: Not everything that everyone does is directly related to you or your actions. Taking things personally is a sure way to see yourself in a negative light. Everyone struggles at times, but this does not mean that the negativity is all your fault. By taking on these burdens, you are putting a lot of unnecessary stress and pressure on yourself. Don't assume that someone is in a bad place because of you unless it is explicitly discussed. This will save you from potentially stressing out over nothing.

You have probably experienced this before, over-thinking to the point where it nearly makes you sick. Maybe you spend hours, or days, thinking about the situation and how you are blaming yourself. Come to find out, there are other factors that have led to this outcome. Perhaps you will hear a confirmation that you are actually not at fault, but merely a bystander. Thinking back on this, you have just spent a substantial amount of time worrying for no reason.

- **Don't Make Assumptions**: Much like the previous tip, you shouldn't make assumptions until you have all of the information possible. Just like you can wrongly assume things based on your directive beliefs, you have a chance of misreading the signs of situations that are happening around you. In an attempt to relieve your stress, you might want to make some assumptions to put yourself at ease.

  This plan typically backfires because your assumptions might run rampant. Because these thoughts are not based on substantial facts, your mind has the ability to focus on only what can go wrong. Listening to information and observing situations without making assumptions can be difficult, but make sure you call yourself out when you notice that you are doing this. It will help you change your view of yourself, instilling more confidence in you.

- **Always Do Your Best**: Giving up before you give a situation a chance is how you set yourself up for automatic failure. Always try your best and give things your all. You will feel better knowing that you tried to do everything possible, using your resources, rather than being overtaken by the idea that you are already going to fail. Trying your best is a habit that will always promote self-growth and self-improvement.

Understand that striving for excellence is a learned habit. You need to give yourself proper motivation so you will keep your momentum going. When you stop trying, this is when you will find yourself in situations where you might start to lose confidence. Push yourself to do better, even when you feel that you have already done everything you can. There are always ways to improve your abilities.

- **Visualization**: The power of visualization is very important. When you visualize the things that you want for yourself and for your life, they will turn into reality. There is no one proper way to visualize your future, but you can try many different ways to see which one works for you. Start off during a time when your mind is clear. This can be when you wake up in the morning or before you go to sleep at night. Make sure that you have some time alone to prevent yourself from getting distracted.

  Picture an outcome that you would like to achieve. Imagine yourself there, happy and fulfilled. See this as a reality that you can achieve. Don't put too much worry behind how you will get there or when, but instead, enjoy how it feels to accomplish this. If you get into the habit of doing this every single day, your mind will transform and get used to relying on positive thinking.

Chapter 2:
Emotions - The Neuroscience of Emotions

We already know that emotions are instinctive feelings that stem from life experiences, but recently, a new take on emotions wants to showcase how emotions are actually concepts. The Theory of Constructed Emotion is presented by psychology professor and neuroscientist Dr. Lisa Feldman Barrett. Her newfound claims contradict the original model that we use to identify human emotions. They argue that emotions are the following:

- Not an ancient thought process in the brain
- Not able to be detected through facial expressions or other physiological measurements
- Not universal with commonalities that are experienced by all people or cultures
- Not belonging to distinctive parts of the brain devoted to specific emotions
- Not reactions to external events

The last 25 years have been spent researching subjects to explain the secrets of the emotional brain further. Dr. Feldman Barrett and her team did this research at Northeastern University by poking and prodding the brains and bodies of thousands of willing participants.

Because the theory revolves around the idea that emotions are actually concepts, it is thought that the brain constructs them by choice. Your brain is always receiving data from many different sources. It can see shapes and colors and beings. After viewing this information, it needs time to process it so it all makes sense. One way that your brain might make sense of things is by recalling past memories or experiences that you've had. This can guide your brain to a conclusion, and it makes it easier if you've seen something similar in the past. Your brain does not have to work as hard to process the information if it is already familiar with it.

This makes a lot of sense, but now consider that your brain would have to sort through hundreds of thousands of old memories to make this a permanent way of functioning and identifying emotions. This would be very time-consuming. Therefore, Dr. Feldman Barrett's theory tells us that the brain uses concepts to save time. She believes that these concepts are compressed versions of old memories and encounters. For example, instead of trying to remember every single car you've seen, your brain will store the concept of a car. The next time you see one driving down the street, your brain recalls that concept, not the entire database of memories where you've seen other cars.

You can think of concepts as categories that your brain makes. This is how you are able to make sense of what is going on around you. If you see something new, your brain does not try to find the origin of the object or event. Instead of asking, "What is this?" your brain will wonder, "What is this like?" It will try to recall a concept of something else that it knows. With this comparison, your brain is constantly trying to perceive information and categorize it. The idea of the brain using conceptualization is not new, but Dr. Feldman Barrett's work helps to unlock more information about it.

Illness and the Body

While you are already aware that your emotions can play a huge role in your mental health, emotions can also greatly impact your physical health. Emotions are directly connected to your body in many ways. They are very powerful, often making you feel certain impacts without you even realizing it is happening. Breaking down a few of the most common emotions, you will see just how powerful they can be when it comes to your physical body.

Love

When you are in love, your heart races. This quickness in pace happens because you are excited or enthralled to be before the one you love. Your hands might even start to get sweaty. This happens because of the adrenaline and norepinephrine being produced. All at the same time, oxytocin, the "love" hormone, is being released into your system. This makes you feel very happy and confident. It is thought that the feeling of love can be enough to heal your pain, as it works in the same way as painkillers do. Because certain areas of your brain are positively activated, your heart also becomes healthier. All around, love is a great feeling that benefits you physically in many ways.

Anger and Anxiety

Both of these emotions impact you similarly. When you are filled with anger, you are usually filled with rage or irritation. This can cause your head to start hurting because you are holding on to so much tension. In some cases, it can also upset your stomach by causing indigestion. When you are angry, you are also stressed. This can lead to skin problems such as acne or breakouts. In severe cases, you might experience a heart attack or stroke. The same symptoms are present when you experience anxiety, but they attack more slowly. Anxiety is not quite as direct as anger, but it can be just as detrimental. When you feel very anxious, you aren't going to feel very comfortable physically. This can cause the same headaches, stomach aches, and health conditions.

Depression

When you are depressed, this increases your risk of developing other illnesses. While depression is a mental illness, it comes with a lot of physical symptoms. For one, it makes your immune system weak. It can also lead to insomnia because you are constantly filled with worry or doubt. Your thoughts can hold a lot of power over you when you are depressed. This discomfort and exposure to stress can lead to serious concerns, like a heart attack. If you are depressed, this can also impact your memory and cause you to have difficulties when faced with decisions.

Fear

When you are fearful, you might notice how it feels like the blood is draining from your face, leaving you hollow. This is actually what happens when you are scared. The blood drains from your face, causing you to grow pale. Because of your fight-or-flight response, this triggers your blood vessels and tells them to stop the blood flow from your face and extremities. It then directs blood flow to your muscles so you are actually able to flee if you need to. This emotion normally causes a very quick physical response. If you are caught off guard, you know how draining it is to feel fear. It often takes some time to recover.

Disgust

This is one of the most difficult emotions to control. When you are disgusted, your body responds quickly. Unlike other emotions that make your heart rate speed up, disgust makes it slow down. You might also feel nauseous as a result of this. A feeling can occur in the pit of your stomach, making it seem like you have to throw up. This happens due to the antipathy in your digestive system. Antipathy is a hormone that has a lot of the same elements as the natural makeup of your digestive system. However, too much of it is what causes you to feel sick. When you do feel disgusted, you can remind yourself to take deep breaths and remind yourself that your emotions are trying to control your thinking.

Shame

Unhealthy shame usually comes from the past and the experiences you've had. In this case, it can become toxic. When you hold on to this kind of shame, it can cause you a lot of stress. This causes problems because your stress hormone, cortisol, will be triggered and over-produced. When this happens, you will experience an increased heart rate and constricted arteries. If you can feel shame coming on, you can stop it by reminding yourself that comparisons are typically unhealthy. If you frequently compare yourself to others and to past experiences, this is going to set you up for the unnecessary stress that toxic shame brings.

Pride and Contempt

When you have unreasonable pride, this feeling stems from negative thoughts about other people mixed with the feeling that you are better than everyone around you. Through the stress that this brings, you might experience heartburn, stomach aches, and high blood pressure. If it is hard for you to say "I'm sorry," you need to evaluate your actions, or else you might experience these negative physical impacts. Holding on to any type of negativity for too long is detrimental to your health.

Jealousy

When jealousy happens in small amounts, it can be an endearing emotion to feel. However, it becomes detrimental if it is too intense. Being very jealous can lead to an unhealthy amount of stress. It can cause you to lose your appetite, lose weight, have trouble sleeping, and experience other stomach-related illnesses. Because you are worrying so much about the possibility of something happening, this translates to a sinking feeling in the pit of your stomach. This discomfort, mixed with mental torture, makes jealousy a difficult emotion to process.

Happiness

It radiates throughout your entire body. When you feel happy, you are better able to overcome stressful situations. Your immune system also becomes stronger to ward off illnesses. Happiness is so beneficial that some studies have even shown that being happy makes you live longer. When you are happy, your whole body is able to relax and feel comfortable. Even if you have pre-existing conditions, happiness has been known to improve your physical pain. Some people get so comfortable when they are happy that they begin sleeping and eating more. By gravitating toward these comforting actions, happiness tends to promote more habits that will lead to additional happiness.

If you never considered the impacts of certain emotions on your health before, you are likely more keen on doing so now. When you hold on to certain emotions, you might be damaging parts of your body without even realizing it. Stress and negativity can do a lot of damage if you aren't careful, so it is always best to check-in and make sure that you are experiencing emotions that you can process and handle. Life isn't perfect, so you are bound to experience negativity sometimes, but this does not mean you should dwell on it and live in a state of discomfort.

You must learn how to process your feelings, listening to your emotions and picking up on the actions that you take when you are in certain moods. It helps to have an understanding of your own traits and behaviors because they aren't necessarily going to be the same as anyone else's. Following the idea that the brain seeks concepts when trying to process information, you are giving yourself a better chance of conceptualizing an emotion by taking time to truly experience it and identify what has caused it. You don't need to feel bad about yourself if you do have negative emotions sometimes. This is a part of life, and you need them to grow as a person.

Mastering Your Emotions

Feeling your emotions is one part of mastering them, but to be in control of how you act when you feel them is the next part. Negative emotions can feel almost impossible to control because they are so powerful. You might feel helpless when you experience certain emotions, but there are ways to regain the control you deserve. To start, you must think about the ways you deal with your negative emotions and why they can possibly hold you back. As you identify what isn't working, you will know which habits to change to improve your life.

Avoidance: If something is unpleasant, you might simply avoid it to prevent yourself from having to deal with it. This can feel like a great plan at first, but this does not fix your problem. You will still have to deal with it, but you are simply delaying the process for yourself. As you avoid negative emotions, you are also avoiding opportunities to grow. In some cases, people use drugs or alcohol to further avoid their negative emotions. These mind-altering substances make it easier to ignore problems and move on from them without dealing with them. Again, this doesn't fix the problems. It simply delays paying attention to them.

Denial: This is a dissociative type of response that normally takes place when something bad is happening. For example, you might feel like you are in denial when you get broken up with because you just can't believe that it is happening to you. Breakups are incredibly painful, and they can be negative. To save yourself some heartache, you might be tempted to just go into denial when your partner tries to bring up a conversation about not seeing each other anymore. This places you in a situation where you are not living in reality, which isn't healthy. Like many other coping mechanisms that mask your emotions, you will still need to face your emotions sometime in the future.

Competition: Some people take on their negative emotions and turn them into personality traits. An example of this is someone who is always trying to one-up another person. If someone experiences hardship, this person might respond with, "Oh, you think you've got it bad? Listen to what is happening to me." This type of competition is not healthy and has no foundation in self-improvement or growth. Instead, it is only going to limit you and keep you from experiencing new opportunities because you are so stuck on the idea that you are miserable.

If you are ready to take on your emotions directly so you can move on with your life, you can use this technique to get you started. While you will learn more techniques later, this one will give you some basic knowledge about how to get to the bottom of your emotions and what to do with them. The next time that you feel negativity setting in, try to follow these steps:

1. **Identify What You're Really Feeling**: When your negative emotions start to kick in, stop to think about what is really happening. If you feel angry, ask yourself if your anger is just an initial reaction to mask another emotion, or if anger is truly what you are feeling. For example, if you are angry at your friend for their inability to support your career and purchase a product you are selling, ask yourself if there are any other feelings present. You might feel secretly insecure because they did not make a purchase to support you. Whether they simply could not afford to buy anything at the moment or if they had no need for the product, analyzing this might make you feel like you are inadequate.

2. **Acknowledge and Appreciate Your Emotions**: No matter what conclusions you come to, taking the above situation as an example, remain thankful for any emotions that come your way. All of them will send you messages to help you work through the situation. Understand that they are going to serve you well if you learn how to interpret them. You can take a look at your emotions to help you process what happened and to learn how to move forward from it.

3. **Get Curious About the Message**: When you get curious, you are going to be better able to master the emotions you are feeling. This is helpful because it will prevent you from potentially experiencing the same negativity again in the future. The more knowledge you have, the more powerful it will feel. You can ask yourself things like, "What else could this mean?" or "What am I willing to do about it right now?" These thoughts will promote actionable steps that you can take.

4. **Get Confident**: One of the most powerful ways to handle your emotions is to feel confident that you can. It is a simple step to take, but it makes a big difference in your end result. Think about the fact that you have successfully handled this emotion in the past. Even if the circumstances are different, you have experienced it before, and you know

you will get through it. Many negative emotions present themselves as impossible feelings to shake, but this isn't true—you will get through the moment. If you handled it in the past, you can handle it now. Think about how much more knowledgeable you are now versus what you knew then. Also understand that if you make the same choices as you did in the past, you will end up with the same or similar results. Don't be afraid to take some risks in an effort to have a different outcome.

5. **Become Certain You Can Do This**: Now that you are getting your confidence in order, you need to tell yourself that you can certainly handle any emotions that come your way. Not only will you get through this moment, but you will be able to better handle them in the future. Think about all of the different ways you've handled this emotion before. Write down three or four of them and evaluate how well each one worked out. When you can take a look at your realistic options, this will help you make better decisions in the future. Something that feels difficult now might not be so bad if you experience it again later. There is nothing wrong with rehearsing plans and mastering them before your emotions get the best of you.

6. **Get Excited**: Knowing that you are making progress with mastering your emotions is a

great feeling. You deserve to be excited and proud of yourself for doing so. Understand that the best time to handle an emotion is as soon as you start to feel it. This prevents you from harboring any negativity inside for too long. When you can get your feelings out right away, you have a better chance of learning from your emotions and understanding why you feel the way that you do. It is much easier to overcome something difficult before it turns into a problem that torments you. This takes practice, but you should feel confident in your ability to learn and grow.

This is one basic technique to get you started with the task of mastering your emotions. Throughout this book, you will receive even more advice on how to make this an effortless process. This technique is great because it is simple, and it works for all situations you encounter. No matter what you are going through, you can break your reaction down into these six steps to better guide yourself through the process of healing and overcoming. Nobody has to approve of the way you approach things because this is an inherently personalized experience. What matters is how you feel. Keep yourself motivated by thinking back on your past experiences dealing with your emotions. Know that you have accomplished so much, and you are still standing. No matter how difficult your life becomes, you have the persistence necessary to get through anything and to work toward living a happier life.

Chapter 3:
Taking Action

Think about all of the things you've learned how to do over the last several years. You have these skills and abilities because of your hard work, not because of some coincidence. The reason you can drive a car, cook your favorite food, and understand how the washing machine works is not simply because you read some information. You learn by doing, by taking action. All of these activities can be researched thoroughly, but they require practice if you want to get better at them. Through living your life so far, you have already learned a valuable lesson—achieving success means taking effective actions to get there.

Reading is a great beginning to your plan of action. By reading about what you plan on doing, this can make you more familiar with the subject and strategies involved. If you wish to read about something to inform yourself and put yourself at ease, there is nothing wrong with that. Know that it is going to take more than this to truly put your plan into action, though. You need motivation and determination to keep making progress in your life.

Having a lot of information on a topic is useless if you do not plan on taking action in some way. When you take action, you are activating this information and using it strategically. You might read hundreds of self-help articles, but they aren't going to change your life unless you apply the tips to your own life.

Taking action makes the advice very real and tangible. You will get the chance to experience it for yourself and see what it can do for the way you are living. Getting into the habit of taking action is helpful because this will slowly dissolve your insecurities. Instead of wishing you could make the advice work for you, the proof comes from taking action and seeing your real results.

When you take action, you are giving yourself the ability to use the process of elimination better. Think back on the last time you felt stressed out. Part of the stress likely stemmed from the fact that you felt there were no options available to ease your stress. If you are genuinely trying a concept that does not work for you, then you can group it into a category of approaches that you know you don't need to try again. This automatically makes things easier for the next time you are feeling this particular emotion. When you have to do less work to figure things out, they become less stressful in the process.

Not only will you be able to eliminate processes that do not work for you, but you will also be able to create habits out of the ones that do when you take action. Change and success are both ongoing occurrences that never end. As long as you wish to live a fulfilling and enriched life, you will always do yourself the honor of looking for ways to make it the best it can be. By understanding that this part does not have an end date, you can take it upon yourself to constantly strive for better habits. Turn your behavior patterns into strong foundations that will carry you through life. No matter what you are going through, having a strong foundation will help you. The hardest part of all this is getting started. Once you do, this will give you enough momentum to keep progressing.

At the end of the day, you feel proud of yourself for the choices you make. When you take deliberate actions, this gives you a chance to admire your efforts. Even if the end result isn't what you thought it would be, or if you haven't yet reached its final form, you can still feel proud of yourself for knowing that you are doing your best. When you only take passive steps, this can provide you with a false sense of accomplishment. After everything you do, ask yourself what difference this action is making toward your overall situation. Is this bringing more positivity into your life? You need to set your focus on this, ensuring that you are making good use of your time and efforts.

Focus and Taking the Right Action

Any time you decide to take action in your life, know that it is going to require effort. This might come in the form of time, energy, or anything in between. You need to make sure that you have your focus set on the right end goals, or else you are only going to waste your time. To restore the necessary balance in your life, pay attention to the actions you are taking and exactly how they are helping you, those around you, and your situation. One of the best ways to feel mentally free of negativity is to maintain a feeling of balance. When this occurs, your life will not feel so uncertain or stressful. Even negative emotions will be seen as temporary, with real solutions.

Deciding to refocus your attention is a wonderful first step to take to ensure that you are taking the right action. As you work through this process, you will need to evaluate what is truly important to you right now. Know that this can change throughout your lifetime. What might have been essential to you last year will not necessarily hold the same relevance today, and that is okay. You need to listen to yourself and determine what is worth fighting for. Work toward the things that you know will make you feel happy, successful, and whole. As you evaluate your life, consider taking these steps to help you decide what is most important to you.

- **Determine What Holds Value**: Think about your life and what you deem valuable. Without judging yourself, write down the first five things you can think of. This is generally a good indication of what is important because these are the things that are in the forefront of your mind. They are likely what you think about when you need the motivation to keep progressing. You can use these five things as the starting point of a model that you will create. As you make choices in your life, it should be apparent that these are five things you don't want to live without. This means you are willing to fight for them or make necessary changes to keep them in your life.

You can think about these things as the backbone of your existence. If one were missing, this would mess up the basic structure of your life. No matter what you choose, understand that people and events have a huge ability to shape your life and your values. Things change, and this is why what might seem important one year isn't as important the next. You grow and you move on, but this doesn't have to be a bad thing. Consider the person you want to become and make sure that your values align with this lifestyle.

- **Decide What Commitments Are Important**: The commitments you make in your life can either help or hurt the things you value most. A commitment is something that you are obligated to do. Whether you hold yourself to these commitments or you are required by someone else to do them, they are still important to consider. Pay attention to the ways in which your commitments interact with your values. While you might value self-care, making commitments to other people and not leaving any time for yourself does not necessarily align with what you value. In this case, you would need to make adjustments to support your need for self-care better.

You can start by thinking about your essential commitments. These are things that you must do because they support your basic need for survival. Some examples are stocking your refrigerator with food so your family can eat and paying your bills so you have a roof over your head. Of course, you cannot do away with the essentials. Next, you can think about the other commitments that you keep that are optional. While they might be very important, you should know that you have more flexibility when it comes to these things.

- **Assess How You Use Your Time**: Think about your daily routine. These are activities that you normally do automatically because you are used to doing them. Just because something has become a part of your routine does not mean that it is the best way to spend your time. Think about which activities and chores impact your five key values. Do they impact them positively? To get these things to align, you must realize that you have the ability to control how much time you spend doing the various parts of your routine. Think about ways you can transform what you do to better align with your current values.

  Pay attention to what you do in your free time, especially. Consider all of the mindless activities you do to kill time. Are there better, more productive, ways to spend this time? Everyone needs a little bit of downtime every once in a while, but this doesn't mean you can't also be productive. Cut down on the amount of time you spend on your phone, checking your emails, and watching TV. While they are great ways to pass the time, they can eventually cause you to feel like you are in a rut.

- **Get Rid of Clutter in Your Life**: Clutter can come in many different forms. It can be the junk that sits in your kitchen drawers, or it can be the thoughts that cloud your mind and distract you from reaching your goals. When you get rid of clutter in every aspect of your life, you are going to notice an overall improvement. If you have not used something material in the last two years, you likely do not need to keep it. Donate it, repurpose it, or get rid of it. Make space for the potential of growth. It is a great feeling to know that you are decluttering your life and making space for more positivity.

If you have emotional clutter, address it. The longer that something goes without being addressed, the more power you are giving it. If you notice that a coping mechanism is no longer serving you, or is serving you negatively, get rid of it. Seek alternatives and other outlets. They are available, as long as you are willing to find them. Talk to people you trust, and let go of the things that happened in your past. Learn from them, hold on to what is valuable, and let go of what still torments you.

- **Spend More Time with People That Matter**: Those you spend your time around end up influencing your life. It is thought that the five people you spend the most time with can even influence your personality traits. It is natural for people to pick up on each other's habits and values when they are in close proximity often. Make sure that you are in good company, only spending time with those who have positive impacts on your life. You should make it a point to surround yourself with supportive and caring people.

As your life evolves, your inner-circle will also evolve. People come and go, but those who make a lasting impact can still influence the way you are living your life. There is nothing wrong with evaluating your social circle to ensure that it is working out to the best of its ability. If you are spending time around someone who does not make you feel great, this is a red flag that you need to address. Explore the reasons why this is occurring and how you can change the situation. This doesn't always mean cutting people out of your life. More often than not, it means you need to sit down and have an honest conversation.

- **Make Time to Be Alone:** Having time for yourself is incredibly valuable. No matter how social you are, you should still treat alone time as a necessity. When you spend time with yourself, you get to make all the decisions. From what you do to how long you spend doing it, this is a great feeling that you deserve to have. You do not need to live your life primarily alone, but making sure that you know how to be alone is important. Many people rely on others so much that they forget how to function without constant help or outside opinions. Become confident in who you are as a person.

  When you are alone, do things that allow you to care for your mind, body, and spirit. You can seek out some creative activities, great for getting to the bottom of any unresolved emotions that might be lurking below the surface. Do things that you've always wanted to do. Being alone is your chance to explore other areas of life. Just a little bit of additional alone time each week can make you surprisingly happy and fulfilled.

How to Take Action

Taking action can seem overwhelming because you might be expecting major changes. Know that the small actionable steps you take are just as valid as the larger ones. By starting small, this allows you to get used to the idea of taking action. Because you don't feel as overwhelmed, you are better able to follow through with your commitments. As you explore the different ways you can do this in your own life, know that focus is a very big component of the process. By focusing on what you'd like to change, you will then be able to apply the proper technique.

Start Where You Are

There is a big misconception that making any type of change in your life involves a big preparation process. You must plan out what you are going to do and how. While this is true to a certain extent, you can't let timing hold you back. There will never be a perfect time to make a change. Most of the time, change happens out of necessity. You want to see a difference, so you commit to making a change. Just because you wait a little while to ensure you are "prepared" does not necessarily mean that it is going to be easier or more successful.

Don't psych yourself out by believing you are not ready to make the change. Most of the time, change can be scary and you will not ever feel ready. Experiencing something new and unfamiliar is bound to cause you slight discomfort, but you need to weigh your options. You can either experience this temporary discomfort, or you can keep living your life exactly the same way and never change the pattern. It does take a certain degree of sacrifice to make changes, but you will know when something is worth your while.

If you are concerned that you need to wait a little while before making your change, know that right now is a perfectly good starting point. See how much progress you can make from this exact point in time. Carefully track your progress to prove to yourself that timing does not matter as much as consistent effort does. As long as you are willing to put in the work, you will make sure that you adapt to any changes you make. You are a resilient and skilled individual who has made it this far in life already. Anything that comes your way is simply a task that must be handled.

Accept your starting point for what it is. If you believe it is imperfect, you are correct! If you knew everything already, you would not need to make any changes. Even the most successful people in the world had their first starting points. Since then, they have made changes that have allowed them to grow exponentially. You can join these ranks by accepting your life and accepting what you have done so far. The best is yet to come when you live a life that is fueled by motivation and desire.

Get Rid of Distractions

Distractions will always be present, no matter what you are doing. Something as simple as background noise can prove to be a huge distraction when you are trying to focus on something important. As you take more action in your life and make more changes, you must also become great at spotting distractions before they impact you. You can do this by asking yourself what you are focusing on when you are completing a task. Are you focusing on what must be done, or is there something else on your mind? A distraction does not have to be physical. As you know, your own thoughts can prove to be a huge distraction.

Before you do anything of importance, make sure that your head is as clear as possible. If something is lingering on your mind, write it down before you begin. Know that you don't have to throw away the thought. Instead, think of it as a temporary removal. Once you put it down on paper, know that you can come back to it after you finish the task that you set out to accomplish. Later on, you can further dissect how you are feeling and what you must do to feel better. You can also find people to talk to about the situation, allowing you to feel less alone and less distracted.

Electronics can be huge distractions, even if you are not the one using them. Get into the habit of putting away your phone when you are having in-person conversations. Even if it is simply in your hand, this becomes a distraction because you might start to wonder about the notifications you are missing. The television can also provide a distraction, especially when it is on in the background. Even if you aren't consciously paying attention to it, your subconscious might still be picking up on everything that is going on. Only keep your television on if you are actively watching it. Otherwise, you are giving yourself a frequent distraction.

Don't think about work when you are at home and cannot do anything about it. One of the biggest distractions comes from taking stress home. While you might have very valid reasons to feel stressed out about your job, know that you cannot do anything about these situations unless you are on the clock. By bringing home these distractions, you are taking away from your personal time and your alone time. Learn how to temporarily let go of your stress, committing to returning to it as soon as you can and when you are feeling refreshed.

Chapter 4:
Failure and Risk (Turning Problems Into Opportunities)

When you encounter problems in your life, this discourages you and prevents you from living your best life. There will always be times when you do not succeed, but this does not mean that your failures will hold you back. You need to learn how to turn these problems into bigger opportunities. When learning how to do this, you must understand how procrastination works and why it happens. This is one of the main problems you will face during this time of personal transformation. In this chapter, the cycle will be broken down. Through each step, you will be able to identify these traits in yourself and in your life.

Procrastination Cycle

We all wish we could procrastinate less. It is a debilitating cycle that prevents us from doing our best and accomplishing what we strive for. This seems to be a universal challenge that we all share as a collective, struggling to break free of the cycle. It can be difficult to pinpoint why procrastination occurs, and yes, it is important to identify the reason. When you know why it is happening, you will have a better chance of breaking the habits and replacing them with more productive ones. Whether you are focusing on something that happened in the past, present, or future, you need to address the issue.

Most likely, you are able to resonate with the following cycle. These are the commonly-experienced steps that lead to that debilitating feeling that you dread when you cannot seem to reach your goals.

1. **Eager and Energized**: Imagine you have a goal of cleaning out your closet. You are feeling great about this goal initially, able to imagine how good it will feel to have more space in your closet and to get rid of items you no longer use. The clutter has been driving you crazy for a long time now.

2. **Apprehension**: As your optimism starts to fade, you think about what it will take to get your closet clean. You imagine sorting through endless items, deciding what you will keep and what you need to donate. You start to realize how much work is going to be involved. It becomes apparent that you need to take action, even when you already have the right intention.

3. **No Action**: You let some time pass, and you still have yet to complete any of the tasks that will get you to your goal of having a clean closet. There are probably many reasons why you haven't started yet. Maybe you wanted to finish watching television, just one show. Or maybe you want to go have lunch with your friend so you have nourishment before you

start. A feeling of panic begins to set in as you realize how much time has already passed with no progress. This can also lead to frustration or irritability.

4. **Flicker of Hope**: You snap out of your bad mood and think that there is still hope. You can still get the task done in the time you have left. Because you left your task unfinished until the last minute, this provides you with some adrenaline.

5. **Fading Quickly**: When you start to think about *why* you didn't take action sooner, you start to lose the hope that you felt earlier. You might even think, "What is wrong with me?" This self-deprecating behavior leaves you feeling discouraged, angry, or sad. It can even lead to resentment for yourself.

6. **Vow to Yourself**: Instead of completing the task, you spend the rest of your available time feeling sorry for yourself. Once the disappointment finally fades away, you vow to yourself that this will *never* happen again. You make a promise that the next time will be different, and you go to sleep knowing that you still have a messy closet to clean.

If you've been stuck in this cycle before, you are not alone! It is a vicious one that can be hard to tame, but there are actions you can take. The next time you feel stuck like this, think about how you want to break these patterns. Make a commitment to yourself that you will do better and get your tasks done.

To begin your new cycle, you need to take better advantage of the sequence of events that naturally occur. During stage one above, you are feeling the most optimistic about completing your task. When you feel this way, you need to make a solid plan that will allow you to reach your end goal. Think about the steps you must take to get there. Give yourself a deadline! Even if there is no need for a deadline, this will keep you disciplined and committed.

Just because you now have a plan and a deadline in place does not mean the end result will automatically be different—you need to put the plan into action. You need to identify your procrastination triggers so you can resist them. For example, if the television is your weakness, turn it off and keep the remote far away from you. Let yourself watch TV as a reward for completing your task. You need this resistance to fight against procrastination. This will give you time to take your first actionable step.

Think about what else you can do to make things easier. Maybe you would work better with some music in the background to encourage you. There are things you can do that will not distract you, but will make the entire process more enjoyable. Seek these things. Think about your results over your comfort. Now is not the time to prioritize self-care because you are in the middle of a plan of action. You will be able to kick your feet up later. Once you follow all of these new steps, you will see how to take better advantage of the cycle. Your new habits will carry you forward, allowing you to reach goal after goal.

Productive Failure

Through research done on mathematical problem-solving in three Singapore schools, a study was done on "productive failure." This is a method that supposedly leads to better results with learning than traditional teaching methods. The idea behind it is that short-term failure will encourage you to solve problems, therefore, leading to long-term success. The groups involved in the study were 7th graders. Each classroom was given a 30-minute pre-test with nine questions on it. The purpose of this was to identify how much each classroom already knew about calculating average speed.

After this, one class began working on lessons about how to calculate the average speed of a moving object. Their teachers lectured them on the topic by explaining the concepts, working through examples, and encouraging questions. After the lecture, the students were given a chance to practice what they had learned with sample problems. For their homework, they were assigned similar questions. This process was done over the course of seven class periods. After hearing about this first part, you are likely thinking that this sounds like an average teaching method.

The next part of the study began to implement the productive failure method. Another class was split into groups, and each group was tasked with solving a complex problem. They were given these problems with no prior lectures or preparation from their teacher. All they had were their peers to rely on. The groups were given two class periods to solve the complex problems. Instead of homework, they were assigned extra problems to work on in class after completing the work as a group.

After their time was up, the students met with each other and the teacher to explain the solutions and strategies they discovered when solving the complex problems. It was only at that point that the teacher confirmed which answers were right and how to correctly solve the problems. Much like the direct instruction group from above, these students also spent the same amount of time learning how to calculate the average speed. Following the completion of these sessions, all students took a 35-minute post-test to show what they had learned.

The post-test scores and the homework scores were then evaluated to see which method seemed to work better. The direct instruction group scored an average of 91.4% on their homework, while the productive failure group performed terribly. They scored an average of 16% when trying to solve the complex problems and 11.5% when trying to solve the individual extra problems they were given. The post-test scores become the interesting part, however. The post-test included both complex and simple problems, which the productive failure group succeeded at. They scored 84.8% on the simple problems, compared to 75.3% by the direct instruction group. For the complex problems, they scored 59.7%, and the direct instruction group scored 42.4%.

Through this study, it is clear to see that the productive failure method has its benefits. Overall, you are absorbing what you need to truly learn the information and succeed in the future. This method is not only for children in classrooms. You can apply it to your life, too. There are times when you might think you need to do more research or have more time to prepare, but this will only lead to procrastination. Sometimes, it is best to dive right into your task. You might fail at first, even get a little discouraged, but you will learn how to thrive. Putting yourself into a situation you are unsure of activates your fight-or-flight response, which can be exactly what you need.

Inspiration Through Failure

Now that you understand the concept behind productive failure, it is time to explore the benefits. If you have never tried the method before, it might not make sense to set yourself up for any kind of failure, even if it is only temporary. In today's society, there is so much pressure on being successful at everything you do. In everything from your career to social media, you will find pressure to be good at what you do and to have admirers. This is just the way that our culture has developed.

Deviating from the norm isn't always seen as a good thing, especially when there is any type of setback involved. To truly appreciate the benefits of productive failure, it helps to know what you can expect.

When trying to accomplish something, it makes sense to seek a solution. By finding a solution, you have supposedly solved the problem. You can use it to make your life better and to reach your goals. On paper, this sounds great and the process should end there. It does not, however. If you are simply given or told a solution without understanding how you arrived there, you aren't going to be able to duplicate it again in the future. Taking the study as an example, the children who were given prompts and shown examples of how to complete the problems were given direct solutions. This allowed them to have confidence through the direct instruction approach. However, when it came time to put their skills to the test, they weren't strong enough because they were taught the solutions and not necessarily how to arrive there.

The productive failure group succeeded because they had no choice but to test different methods and strategies to come to their own solutions. Through this process, they were encouraged to explore and experiment. The same can be said for life as a whole—getting stuck in a routine feels safe, but it does not promote growth. When you are in a situation you are unfamiliar with, this promotes more growth than even the most focused regular approach. This happens because you must come up with your own ideas to arrive at the goal. You need to think critically and efficiently if you want to succeed. It is important to do things in life that will activate this part of your brain, as most things have become monotonous and automatic.

We live in an age where there are products and services that will do the problem-solving for us. While they seem incredibly helpful in the moment, they are taking away our ability to reason and think critically. To completely transform the way you think, you need to place yourself in more situations that encourage you to do your best. Through having to fend for yourself, you will learn a lot more than simply going through the motions of the same routines that you are already used to.

To get started with this process, you can turn something very simple into a problem to solve. Navigate your way into a nearby town that you are unfamiliar with. Stop there to grab a bite to eat, and then turn off your navigation system on the way home. You must find your way home without using a map. This might be difficult or very easy, depending on how well you do with reasoning and thinking on the spot. By looking at landmarks and reading road signs carefully, you will rely on your in-the-moment decisions to get home. Along the way, you might make a few wrong turns or get lost, but this is part of the productive failure process. By the time you make it home, you will know how to get home in the future if you decide to visit that town again.

You can break down many areas of your life in this way to undo all of the automatic responses or reactions. A simple reversal of the system allows you to become a better problem-solver and encourages you to think for yourself. During this process, you might even become inspired by your own actions. It is okay to feel this admiration for yourself, as you deserve it. Feel proud of the way you are able to dissect information and come to your own conclusions—this is a wonderful trait to have.

Problem Solving

While we are on the topic of dismantling automatic processes, we can take a look at your problem-solving skills. When you encounter a problem, you can think of it as much more than just an opportunity to seek a solution. Your problems can become opportunities if you know how to use them to your advantage. By taking control of the things that try to control you, your problems won't seem like burdens any longer. You have the ability to create many great opportunities for yourself that have always been there. All it takes is a change in perspective to make sure that you are taking full advantage of them.

Think of Yourself as a Full-Time Problem-Solver

When trying to get into the habit of solving problems, you need to convince yourself that you have what it takes at all times. Think of yourself as capable of solving any problem, at any time. The most successful people constantly think of ways to better their lives and the situations that happen to them. Settling for what you have can feel comfortable, but it won't promote any self-growth. You need to aim for something bigger if you want to be able to find new ways to get there.

Think of yourself as a leader in all that you do. Even if you aren't technically in a leadership role, you can still be a leader in the way you live your life. Leaders choose what happens to them rather than waiting for what comes next. If you are actively seeking better solutions to the problems you face, you are going to find more opportunities for yourself. This process does not take much work to get started. It all just depends on your mindset.

Know When to Pivot

You can only play it safe for so long before you reach a crossroads. Life is going to be full of difficult choices to make, but you should know that you can only do your best. Based on what you know and what you've experienced, you need to place as much confidence in yourself as possible. Believe in your ability to make the right choices that will lead you to the results you crave. If you enter the situation full of doubt, the outcome is going to match this uneasy energy.

There will be times when you must change your course of action. Things change and there are external factors involved, but that does not mean you need to abandon your original plan. Having flexibility is a sign that you are a great leader. Being able to pivot means you need to change your immediate actions, yet you are still working toward the same goal. Pivoting is not an indication that you are failing. It is simply another way to get to the goal that you set for yourself. It is important to let go of your pride if you must do this because holding on to it might make you resistant. Remind yourself that staying humble will get you further.

Listen to What Others Have to Offer

You won't always be able to get help with your problems, but when the opportunity is available, don't be ashamed to take it. Other people aren't always going to help you by solving your problems for you. They might be able to offer you some advice or resources that they learned through their own experiences. Always remain open to what others might want to offer you because you never know how much easier this could make your life. When you are open to such an offer, you will learn something new. Even if it does not get you to your goal, it will help you by giving you the knowledge you didn't have before.

Seeing situations that you are familiar with from a different viewpoint can change your entire approach. When you know how to solve a problem by using your own life experiences, this can limit you if you aren't willing to branch out. Think about other possibilities and what might happen if you had other skills. You won't know until you try something new, so it is best to keep an open mind when you are working on solving any type of problem.

Learn From Your Mistakes

You are going to make mistakes in your life; this is inevitable. Nobody is perfect, and mistakes are not always negative. If you can learn something from where you messed up, this mistake turns into a valuable lesson that will help you in the future. The next time you encounter the same situation, you will be better prepared to handle it with ease. Be forgiving when you make a mistake because there is no use in holding a grudge against yourself. Doing so will only make you feel bad and even less willing to try again. You need to boost your morale after a mistake is made, not make yourself feel worse.

Admitting you are wrong can be incredibly difficult. No one wants to admit this, especially to themselves. Understand that you still have a lot to learn, though. When you are wrong, this provides you with a learning opportunity. You will be able to think about what happened, consider alternative options, and try again. This type of resilience and flexibility are both important traits to have when you aim to be a successful leader. Understand that this is what it takes to transform your life.

A Short message from the Author:

Hey, are you enjoying the book? I'd love to hear your thoughts!

Many readers do not know how hard reviews are to come by, and how much they help an author.

I would be incredibly thankful if you could take just 60 seconds to write a brief review on Amazon, even if it's just a few sentences!

Thank you for taking the time to share your thoughts!

Your review will genuinely make a difference for me and help gain exposure for my work.

Chapter 5:
Appreciation & Expectation

If you want to live a happy life, it is important to know when to ditch the comparisons. We all do it—compare ourselves to those we wish we could be like. Whether the other person is more successful or more charismatic, it becomes an unhealthy goal to become just like them. What gets lost in the process is the appreciation you have for yourself. This, mixed with high expectations that will often never be met, can destroy your self-confidence. Breaking free of this trap can make you happier. By putting yourself first, you will be able to understand what is only noise meant to distract you.

"Comparison is the death of joy." —Mark Twain

Getting caught in this trap kills joy because it forces you to disconnect from your inner truth. Perhaps you dream of being an artist, but pressure from your siblings gets in the way. Instead, you feel inclined to attend a medical school like they all did, conforming to a mold that you don't even necessarily want to fit. This is how you rob yourself of opportunities and happiness. Your goals matter, even when they don't appear to be like everyone else's. Individuality is what makes you unique and special.

In today's society, there are a lot of illusions present. When we are feeling unsure of ourselves, it becomes easy to open up to the idea that others hold the key to our happiness. If only we could be more like them, then we would be happy. If we just model our behavior after these influencers and celebrities, we will be successful. It becomes difficult to live your truth when you stray so far from it. Buying into a lifestyle that seems wonderful for someone else can trick you into thinking that it will also be wonderful for you.

Abundance has a different meaning to each person you ask. One person might see an abundant life as having many material possessions, while another might see it as having a big family. You need to define your own meaning of the word, staying true to this goal as you live your life. If you want to live a life where you focus on your artistic abilities and turn them into a career, then that's your truth. Just because other people choose to take different paths does not mean yours isn't important or valuable. You need to do what makes you happy, or else you will end up feeling disappointed when you do reach your goals.

Now is your time to say goodbye to all of the comparisons you hold yourself to. Learn that positivity is going to bring you far more results than being a copy-cat of someone else's life. In a few ways, you can ensure that you are finally letting go of these harmful comparisons and focusing on yourself.

There Is Enough Happiness for Everyone

Happiness is not limited to a number or amount. Anyone can obtain it, as long as they know how. Just because everyone around you is already happy and living a life of abundance does not mean you've missed the quota. This can also be you. Instead of focusing on what everyone else is doing, you must turn your focus inward. Ask yourself what you truly want from life and how you plan on obtaining it.

Your Feelings Will Guide You

All you need to do is pay attention to see where your feelings will take you. When you are doing something that isn't fulfilling or promising, you aren't going to feel happy or proud. You need to find the things that bring you joy, and this comes with a lot of trial and error. Explore your options to better understand what you want from your life. By listening to your feelings, you might uncover new skills and ideas you never knew you had an interest in.

Aim to Encourage

Comparison is a different feeling than inspiration. When you compare yourself to someone else, this is not how you gain inspiration from them. Instead, this makes a direct comparison of the two of you in a competitive way. Not only can this damage your psyche, but it can also damage theirs. For example, if you compare yourself to someone else and talk to them about it, they might start to see themselves as inadequate. One of the best ways to stay happy on your own path is to celebrate the successes that other people experience. Be happy for them, and know that their success will not take away from your own. Being open to encouragement will prevent jealousy from developing, as well.

Virtue and Kindness

Kindness is a very important part of showing your appreciation for other people. The world will always benefit from having more kindness, as people generally like to make enemies and compete with one another. It is essential to understand that lifting one another up is going to make everyone a lot happier in the end. The way you treat people says a lot about who you are as a person. If you are unwilling to celebrate others' success, this shows that you are likely insecure about your own abilities or accomplishments. It is okay to feel this way, but it is not okay to take it out on others.

A rule to remember is that you must give what you wish to receive. If you are not nice to other people, yet you still expect kindness in return, you are going to be met with a lot of disappointment when things do not go your way. It is much wiser to become allies with other successful people rather than enemies. When you can work together, this connection can be beneficial for both of you. Instead of plotting to ruin one another's success, you can combine your efforts and reach even more goals. Consider how you have been treating people lately. Would you be okay if someone else treated you the same way?

Aside from allowing you to feel great mentally, being kind also benefits your physical health. There are many science-backed reasons as to why it pays to be kind.

- **Kindness Releases Feel-Good Hormones**: When you do nice things for people, this releases serotonin in your brain. Serotonin is a neurotransmitter that gives you a feeling of satisfaction and well-being. In the same way that exercise fills you with a rush of endorphins, so can being kind. These are two great hormones that will benefit you by making you happy and making you feel accomplished. The next time you are nice to someone else, understand that you don't feel great about it by coincidence. There are actually chemical changes happening in your brain that promote your happiness.

- **Kindness Releases Anxiety**: Anxiety is a common human experience that varies in severity. Whether you get a little nervous in crowds or become so anxious that you feel you cannot get out of bed, your anxiety is valid. There are many natural ways to reduce the anxiety you feel, and being kind is one of them. When you are nice to someone, this shifts the focus from yourself. Instead of obsessing over the internal feelings you might be struggling with, you will get to turn your focus on someone else. Based on a study done by the University of British Columbia, social anxiety is associated with low positive affect. They also found that those who engage in kind behaviors on a regular basis are better able to raise their positive affect, allowing them to feel less anxious and more engaged in life.

- **Kindness Is Good for Your Heart**: You might notice a warm feeling in your heart when you do something nice for someone else. This is much more than a sensation you get. It is actually a sign that you are feeling oxycontin in your blood vessels. This hormone causes the release of nitric oxide, which expands your blood vessels. This is protective for your heart because it lowers your risk of clotting and clogged arteries. It also effectively lowers your blood pressure. The next time you get this feeling in your heart, appreciate that it is actually making your heart healthier, not only happier.

- **Kindness Can Help You Live Longer**: It is thought that you are at greater risk of heart disease if you do not have a strong network of kind people in your life. Based on the scientific evidence above, it makes sense that your heart is not as strong when you do not have enough kindness in your life. Therefore, being kind and receiving kindness can help you live a longer life. It is a very simple characteristic to look for in another person and to give another person, but it makes a big difference in your quality of life. If you operate with a lot of anger in your heart, you are going to start feeling its physical impacts.

Give yourself a break and open your heart to kindness instead.

- **Kindness Is Great for Reducing Stress**: Stress can often be unavoidable in life. There is always so much to do and many places to be. From work to family life, you might feel that you never get a break. Did you know that being kind can help alleviate your stress? When you help other people, this allows you to focus on the lives of others, which will take the focus away from all of your stress. Even if it is only for a moment, letting go of your stress will greatly improve your health. The tension you are holding on to will melt away, leaving you feeling better equipped to handle your stress again in the future. Affiliative behavior, or prosocial behavior, is thought to give you the ability to cope with stress. This means the more you engage with others and are kind to them, the better you will feel when it comes to functioning under stress.

- **Kindness Prevents Illness**: Inflammation is a silent culprit that is responsible for many health issues. This can lead to cancer, diabetes, chronic pain, obesity, and migraines. In a study done on adults aged 57-85, those who volunteered their time experienced lower levels of inflammation than those who did not. As you already know, you are able to experience the benefits of oxycontin when you are kind. This hormone is known for reducing inflammation in your body and brain. It acts as a way to protect you from potential illnesses that tend to develop when you are unhappy.

Another aspect of kindness comes from your ability to forgive. When you hold on to grudges and have resentment in your heart, this puts a lot of stress and pressure on you. Even if something happened a long time ago, holding on to it now will continue to affect you. Being able to forgive and move forward is essential if you want to be truly happy. You need to address the situation, make any necessary amends, consider the lesson learned, and strive for a better future. Those who frequently hold grudges find themselves unhappy more often than not. This occurs because holding on to any kind of negativity will impact your daily life.

If you have unresolved feelings that are making you unhappy, you need to get to the bottom of them. Talk them through with someone you trust, or have a mature discussion with someone you used to butt heads with. This process isn't always going to be easy, but it is necessary to truly forgive and move forward. Know that forgiving yourself is just as important. If you are living with regrets because of the decisions you made in the past, you need to address those too. No matter what happened, you cannot change the past or go back in time. The only time you have is now, so you must make the most of it. Learn from your mistakes and understand that you are only human.

Gratitude: A Guide

It can be easy to forget how to be thankful. When life becomes busy and full, you get used to the wonderful things all around you. Expressing gratitude is important because you need to keep yourself humble. When you learn how to appreciate, and be thankful for, the things you already have, you will be able to live a much happier life. Expressing gratitude does not have to be a complex process. In fact, there are many ways you can do it daily that you can incorporate into your regular routine.

- **Don't Be Picky**: You don't have to wait for a big moment of victory to express gratitude. Being thankful for even the smallest things will allow you to practice gratitude on a regular basis. Be thankful for each new day you get, the chance to fill your hours with the things that make you happy and fulfilled. Appreciate the people you have in your life, the way they support you and treat you with kindness. Feel pride in the job you have and the hard work you put into it. You can even express gratitude for things like short grocery store check-out lines or no traffic on your way home. Nothing is too small to be acknowledged and appreciated.

- **Find Gratitude in Challenges**: The trick to becoming great at expressing gratitude comes with the lesson that gratitude is not only reserved for positive experiences. While this is how it is traditionally celebrated, you must open your eyes to the lessons you learn from negative experiences. Difficult situations have a way of bringing forward all the things you feel thankful for. When you have a hard day at work with difficult clients, it might help you to remember that you have a wonderful family waiting to eat dinner with you at home. What starts as negative does not always have to end the same way. You can take a closer look at past negative experiences you've had to identify what you are thankful for. Based on the lesson you learned, what got you from point A to point B?

- **Practice Mindfulness**: Get into the habit of practicing mindfulness daily. Sit down at the end of each day and think about five to 10 things you are grateful for. They can range from material items to people to situations. When you do this daily, you will be able to program your brain to always think this way, seeking out the good in your life. It is thought that it only takes about eight weeks of practicing gratitude to change your thought patterns. Consider your brain a powerful tool that you can use to help you become happier. Know that the more you practice mindfulness, the more you will start to display empathy to those around you.

- **Keep a Gratitude Journal**: After each mindfulness session you have, it is a great addition to journal your feelings. Fill this journal with positive thoughts about what you just reflected on. By keeping track of these things now, you will be able to look back at your journal during times when you need some motivation. You will be reminded of the things that bring you happiness, encouraging you to break free from the constraints that negative thinking places on you. Try to write in your gratitude journal on a regular basis. Even if you don't get around to writing in it daily, aim for a weekly date where you take some time for yourself to write. This will become another great habit to keep the gratitude flowing.

- **Volunteer**: The way you spend your time says a lot about the kind of person you are. In life, balance is always necessary. If you spend too much time focused on yourself, you might become riddled with negativity and challenges. Taking some time to care for other people will help you. When you give back to other people, this increases your own well-being. A study done by the University of Pennsylvania professor, Martin Seligman, shows that volunteering is the single most reliable way to increase your well-being. Helping others truly helps you! There are many volunteer opportunities that you can take advantage of. Do some research and see which options appeal to you most. Don't limit yourself to just one—you can try out many different volunteer opportunities.

- **Express Yourself**: This is a way to express gratitude to the people around you. It is easy to think great thoughts about what you have in your life, but when was the last time you showed verbal appreciation for your spouse or best friend? An experiment was done that encouraged people to write letters expressing gratitude to loved ones expressing gratitude. After sending the letters, the participants' happiness increased by 4%. However, the participants were then instructed to make phone calls to express their gratitude. This increased their overall happiness by 19%. Never underestimate the power of talking to someone you care about. It will make you feel better. After getting into this habit, you will be able to consistently raise your happiness levels, keeping you in a great mood.

- **Spend Time with Loved Ones**: Taking the above suggestion to another level, you can arrange to spend time in-person with your loved ones. Being around great people lifts your mood almost instantly. When you must pay attention to the person in front of you, what you are doing, and what you are talking about, this allows you to let go of the problems that plague you. Even if this is a temporary feeling, it should uplift you enough to move forward from what you are experiencing. If you don't know what to do or say when you are spending time with loved ones, start with a compliment. This is one way to lighten the mood and spark a conversation.

- **Improve Happiness in Other Areas of Life**: While being grateful makes you happy, experiencing happiness also makes you grateful. The two come together to bring a wave of positivity into your life. If you are unhappy about your job, your relationship, or your family dynamic, you need to take a look at the other areas in your life. Aside from the area you are having trouble with, focus on the rest, and make those even better. When you can build up the other sources of happiness in your life, this will outweigh what you are struggling with. It will also give you the encouragement necessary to fix what is wrong. For example, if your boss has been giving you a hard time lately, focus on the dynamic you have with your spouse and family. This should uplift you, reminding you that you still have a lot to be grateful for.

Chapter 6:
The Present Moment

You are familiar with the idea that you must live in the present, as you cannot change the past and the future is yet to happen. Living in the present is important and in this chapter, you will learn why it will make you happier to do so. To do this, it takes focus. It is a lot harder than it seems, especially when you have a lot of other things happening in your life as a result of the past and the future. To live in the present, you need to momentarily block everything else out so you can focus. For example, when you are washing the dishes after dinner, pay attention to your task. Look at the pile of dishes and know that your goal is to clean them all. Focus on getting each plate, cup, fork, and spoon clean. Carefully lay them all out to dry. Once you have completed the task, you can go back to your other thoughts.

When you live this way, you are able to put more effort into what you are presently doing. This means that you will be less likely to mess up or take shortcuts that will only lead to more work in the future. If you were thinking about what you have to do at work the next day as you wash the dishes, you might become distracted by the stress and miss that you weren't properly cleaning some of the plates. After you finished up, it would feel discouraging to see that some of them were still dirty, requiring you to rewash them. When you focus on the present, you put your mind at ease. Not only does this make your life easier, but the simplicity also makes it better.

Being present means your mind needs to be engaged in the task in front of you at all times. This applies during instances that involve others, as well. If you are on a first date, you need to be focusing on the person on the other side of the dinner table. Do not let your mind wander back in time to your ex and how the two compare. Also, do not let your mind daydream about your other options on other dating apps. If you are in the moment, you are giving the experience a fair chance. Your distractions might prevent you from realizing that the person in front of you is wonderful and a great match. This tends to happen a lot because of society's multitasking culture.

People are taught that doing more at once equates to productivity. While this might be true if you are working on tasks at your job, it often does not translate the same way when it comes to your personal life. You should not split your time up too much when you are dealing with matters of the heart or even friendship. This becomes unfair because you are only giving part of your attention to the person you are interacting with. Either focus on them or do not get involved in the interaction at all. By changing this habit, you will better appreciate the qualities that the person or situation brings into your life.

To commit to the present, ask yourself the following questions:

- Is my mind where my body is right now?

- What can I feel in my body right now?
- What is perfect about this situation?
- What sensations do I feel in my body?
- What is my breathing like?

These questions will activate your brain and urge it to become focused on the present. Oftentimes, we are waiting for the next thing to happen. This means we aren't enjoying the present, what is happening right now. It is customary, in today's society, to think about what is to come and why we should look forward to it. While having these goals and aspirations is great to a certain degree, you can't forget to live in the moment; enjoy what you have right now.

Space-Time and Time-Space

The way that you view the world gives you a concept of what you deem valuable and important. Your worldview influences you on a daily basis, encouraging you to either take action or stay where you are. In this section, we are going to take a look at two different concepts. These worldviews have been widely used for the last century, and having a better understanding of them might inspire you to change the way you see the world.

Newtonian World

Otherwise known as the mechanistic worldview, the Newtonian world operates through reductionism, determinism, materialism, and a reflection-correspondence view of knowledge. It is a simple and coherent concept. However, it denies a few core elements that a lot of people tend to use in their worldviews. Some of these things include creativity, evolution, human agency, and values. Until the early 20th century, Newton developed classic mechanics, which was seen as a foundation for science. It was predicted that future scientists would have other findings, but ultimately, their findings would be reduced back to the same classical mechanistic principles.

When most people think about the term "scientific thinking," they use it interchangeably with "Newtonian thinking." The science behind his way of thinking is fairly simple to follow. He believed in reductionism; this implies that understanding any complex phenomenon means that you must take it apart first. Once you can identify its components, you will be better able to identify it as a whole. If you are still unable to make any sense of it, you can further reduce each component until you understand how they work together.

If you continue the reduction process, you will only be left with atoms to observe. The Newtonian principle believes that any phenomena is materialistic. This includes items, biology, social matters, and mental matters. This logic is simple and easy to follow, though it is minimal. Through Newtonian logic, an agent should always choose the option that best maximizes its utility. Because of this, it is believed that actions of the mind are deterministic (predictable). This means that there is a sense of linear progress: an increase in global utility means more increases in scientific progress. This theory does not account for free will and chance. It states that every decision made is deliberate and purposeful, even if the agent does not realize it.

Many people do not identify with this theory because of the denial of creativity and values. According to this worldview, human actions are mainly predictable. We should make choices that will most benefit us at the moment. The Newtonian worldview does not believe that spontaneous decisions or moments of inspiration have an impact on our actions. In the end, we are only operating based on what we know we need to do, even if this knowledge is subconscious. With this theory, there is little room to explore chance and coincidence. It is as though everything can be explained in a Newtonian world.

For some, the Newtonian worldview brings them peace and understanding. Because everything can be calculated and explained, there is little to fear. Even when bad things happen, it can be said that they happened for the purpose of the greater good. You're familiar with the saying, "Everything happens for a reason." While the world might be full of seemingly complex situations and concepts, Newtonian thinking boasts simplicity. When you break down the components of these complex situations, it is possible to see things in a more simplistic worldview that is easier to explain, process, and accept. Once you break everything down, it is thought that the course of evolution will remain predictable, and even reversible. Any knowledge you gain is meant to come to you, through a pre-existing path that has been created before you even knew it existed.

Quantum World

Quantum mechanics is the theory of all things microscopic. This tiny world consists of particles, atoms, and molecules that can explain much larger phenomena. In a Quantum world, radioactivity and antimatter can be explained while observing how its particles behave on small scales. Another element of the theory of the Quantum world is that Quantum objects can exist in multiple states. This means that they can be in different places at the same time. This theory is full of uncertainty and paradoxes, much more abstract than the Newtonian theory we just learned about. There is a big question regarding objective reality and if it even exists. In the past, great minds such as Albert Einstein had a problem accepting this theory.

Today, scientists are still trying to make sense of it all by attempting to harness all of its bizarre properties. Quantum theory started in the 20th century. It came about when other ideas were unable to explain certain concepts. Other theories suggested that atoms vibrated at any frequency, which led to incorrect predictions. Max Planck, in 1900, changed this assumption by proving that atoms only vibrate at certain frequencies. In 1905, Einstein further expanded on this point by showcasing that light came in packages of energy called photons. Light was then seen as a sort of chameleon, with the ability to behave as either a particle or a wave.

In 1927, Werner Heisenberg formulated a theory that states there is an upper limit on the knowledge we have. It suggests we can never truly know the position and momentum of a quantum object because one can change with the other. This theory can be explained with the notion of entanglement. It's the idea that, in the Quantum world, objects are no longer able to operate independently if they have interacted with each other. Those particles they interact with now have a say in what happens to them. After they become linked, they can continue to impact each other, even at a distance. Einstein used to refer to this as "spooky action at a distance."

Entanglement can be used to explain a concept that we are very familiar with today—communication. Quantum cryptographers can send "keys" to decode encrypted information. The process of unlocking it is based on using Quantum particles. If these particles are intercepted along the way, it will disturb their Quantum state and that will then be detected by the cryptographers. If you are picking up on this concept, you will be able to see how this explains the art of cybersecurity that we use today. Computer networks are encrypted to keep all of the information safe from hackers.

Many scientists believe that the Quantum world can be used to explain countless problems that we will encounter in the years to come. It has already opened up a whole world of ideas that can be built upon. When people are able to harness the power of Quantum power, this shows great promise for the future of the technological world. These particles are so tiny that they cannot be detected by the human eye. It requires science and technology to make sense of it all. This, combined with the idea that Quantum particles can obey Quantum rules if they do not become entangled, will continue to lead to many great developments. There is nothing that is very predictable or simplistic about this worldview, especially when it comes to entanglement.

Unbiased Thought

To better understand how to stay present, you must take a look at your thoughts. Are they biased and being made to lead you to certain actions? Having an unbiased thought process shows you are able to live in the present. It can be incredibly difficult to train your brain to focus in this way. Most of the time, our thoughts are racing. Our heads become filled with things that we wish we could do, what we think we should do, and ideas that expand on other thoughts that are left. It can all become very overwhelming and hard to focus if you do not have a way to sort through it all. These thoughts can also begin to impact our future actions, most of the time without us realizing it.

For example, if you have a conversation with a friend about their partner who does not meet their needs, this will influence your thoughts. You might have a wonderful partner with a keen sense of what you need to be happy, but in your subconscious, holding on to these other thoughts can influence your actions. If your partner does something that upsets you by mistake, you might judge them harshly because of the thoughts you were exposed to when you talked to your friend. This can lead to problems because it escalates situations, even if you don't intend for it to. Many people are left wondering why they are so unhappy and why their social interactions are often misunderstood. A purging of their innermost thoughts can prove to be helpful, in this case.

Meditation is a helpful tool when it comes to emptying your mind. When you meditate, you are pulling up the roots of all the things that are on your conscious and subconscious mind. By identifying each thought, you will be able to understand what to let go of and what you can allow inside. Through guided meditation, you will find ways to successfully complete this progress while simultaneously relaxing. With Jon Kabat-Zinn's guided meditation, you can practice this process until you feel mentally sound.

1. In a dimly lit and quiet room, get yourself situated on the floor or a comfortable flat space. Lying on your back, close your eyes gently. Make sure that you aren't straining to force them closed. Allow your eyelids to settle into place, relaxing into the feeling. Ride each wave of breath, paying attention to its speed and frequency. Have an awareness

of your entire body, allowing it to express itself moment-by-moment.

2. When you feel ready, let go of your body and your breath. Allow it to drift into the background of your mind, understanding that it will continue to operate, even if you don't have all of your attention on it. Trust that your body knows what to do. Allow your thoughts to enter the stage, the new foreground of your mind.

3. Recognize that a stream of thoughts has probably entered now. Don't allow it to carry you away, but acknowledge that it exists. Rest comfortably on the riverbank, seeing each thought passing by. Let them be acknowledged individually, proving that you are not being biased toward any thoughts in particular.

4. Take a look at these thoughts as mental events. With each one, your brain needs to process it and determine if action must be taken. It is a whole process that depends on the content of the thought. There is no right or wrong way to operate, as your thoughts are all diverse and interesting on their own.

5. As the thoughts pass you by, see them as bubbles in the water. They might get carried downstream, even popped. Accept this process as they move through your mind. No matter the urgency or the content, each thought is still a part of the overall stream.

Understand that pleasant and unpleasant thoughts operate in the same way.

6. Expand the metaphor by imagining the thoughts as clouds in the sky now. They might linger briefly, but eventually, they will dissipate and become very far removed from you and your life. You accept this process because it is natural and beautiful. You know that other clouds will continue to fill the sky. Try to relate all of these thoughts in equal regard. From what you ate for lunch to what your child last spoke to you, understand that these thoughts are each full of information that impacts you.

7. Allow all of your thoughts to come and go as they please. Think of them as something fluid that is in motion. Pay attention to the sounds and sensations, as your thoughts might take on each of these forms. Accept them for what they are and how they make you feel. Take advantage of the restful spaces in between each thought.

8. Think of yourself as being on the outside of this situation. Understand that you can turn down the noise at any time, as you would the volume on a television. Know that you are just watching and listening without the need to be completely immersed in what is going on all over again. Give yourself the chance to experience your thoughts without being

upset or impacted by them like you were the first time you thought about them.

9. Without being pulled back into your past, learn that it is okay to think about what has happened while being void of intense emotion. While the event or situation can still hold importance in your life, know that you do not have to commit yourself to it every time you think about it. Understand that your reactions to these things are mental events, not necessarily facts. When you come from a biased point of view, your emotions lead the way.

10. Pay attention to how easily your thoughts can lead to the transformation of your views, opinions, beliefs, plans, and actions. If you feed into each thought, becoming immersed in them again, your mind is more likely to become influenced by them. The more that you practice this habit, the easier it is to do this without even thinking.

11. If you need to, come back to this peaceful moment over and over. Experience what it feels like to be slightly removed from your thoughts, simply observing. Understand that this is not only acceptable but healthy for you to experience.

12. As you take each breath, feel how aware you are at this moment. Take up residence in your awareness, recognizing that it is a powerful position to hold. Change your

narrative to become more accepting of your thoughts and feelings, whatever their content or emotional value may be.

13. If you take an observational approach, you will be less likely to automatically take on the many burdens your thoughts can bring you when you don't need to. See your thoughts as something vast, such as a weather pattern. Know that they will fluctuate and waver at times. Appreciate how you no longer feel imprisoned by any of your thoughts.

14. For the remainder of your meditation, stay centered and peaceful. Allow your thoughts to flow freely while reminding yourself that you are simply observing them as they pass through. Let them come to you without seeking a deep, emotional connection to them.

15. Know that you can keep using this strategy, even beyond this meditation. You can take your thoughts by the moment, as they come to you.

This adaptation of Mr. Kabat-Zinn's meditation should put you in a wonderful place emotionally. You can use it anytime you feel that there is too much noise going on in your head. To follow the meditation auditorily, you can find it here:

https://www.mindful.org/a-meditation-on-observing-thoughts-non-judgmentally/

Chapter 7: Actionable Steps to Change Your Mind

Meditation is one of the most valuable tools you can use to transform your life. By working from within, you will understand how to better reframe your thoughts in a positive way to better suit your life and what happens in it. These actionable steps will give you the framework to better yourself as a person and to unlock many new opportunities that you didn't know existed before you. With this newfound knowledge, you will have a better way to cope with your emotions when they become too much for you to handle.

Guide to Meditation

There truly isn't a "right" way to meditate, but there are some basic foundations you can follow to ensure you will receive the most from your experience. Meditation is a way to relax and listen to your innermost thoughts. By sorting through them, you will better understand what you are feeling and what you should do next. No matter what type of meditation you seek, set aside some time for this in your schedule. When you make time for it, you will take it more seriously and work to prevent distractions from interrupting you. Know that your meditation will not serve you well if you are constantly being distracted by people in the room, background noise, or other busy environmental circumstances.

You don't need to meditate for an hour a day to feel the benefits. Even setting aside just a few minutes will get you started on a positive path to a healthy habit. Regular practice is important when it comes to mediation, as it is a skill that is learned. The more you practice, the better you will get and the more it will benefit you. Much like any other skill you practice, you will become more familiar with it the more you do it. Mindfulness meditation does not involve letting your thoughts run wild. It teaches you how to identify them by being present and self-aware. Another misconception is that you need to empty your mind completely. While it might feel empty at times, there are usually plenty of thoughts inside to be addressed.

Your mind is going to roam; you can expect this. Don't feel bad if this happens because this is a normal part of the meditation process. You might also notice other sensations, like the tendency to daydream about the future or the reflection of your past coming to the surface. Know that all of these experiences are natural and part of the human experience. If this happens during your meditation, simply pause and reset your focus. Let the thought enter your mind and then let it exit. You can then focus back on centering your breath and relaxing your body.

You can meditate at any time, anywhere. Listen to yourself and notice when you might benefit most from meditating. A lot of people enjoy doing this after they wake up or right before they go to sleep. These are usually the times when the mind is most relaxed. You can do it on your own, or you can listen to a guided meditation. It can be helpful to follow along with a guided meditation in the beginning to give you some direction. This also allows you to know when you should start coming back to the awareness of being in the present, which can be hard to do when you are inexperienced.

Along with steadying your breathing, don't forget about your body while you are meditating. You can use the "body scan" method to ensure you are relaxing as much as possible. By focusing on different areas of your body, starting from your head to your toes, you can make sure that each part is relaxed and peaceful. It becomes easy to hold on to tension when you know you must be still for an extended period of time. Your brain might try to fight this at first.

It is common to experience sensations such as tingling or itching in your body because your mind might be telling it to keep moving. In today's world, it is so common to feel the pressure of the need to be productive and to do more. Meditation allows you to unwind some of this pressure, letting you just be. It is important for everyone to feel this sense of relief every once in a while. When tensions are high, this leads to more negativity and conflict in life.

No matter if your meditation is themed to focus on a certain subject or free-roaming, you can experience the same wonderful benefits. After you meditate, you should feel an immense sense of clarity and peace about yourself and your life. Know that you can listen to your mind and body to determine how much meditation you need. Never force yourself to meditate when you know you aren't going to give it your all or your attention. This will simply be counterproductive. Save your meditation for a time you will commit to it.

Walking Meditation

In a general sense, walking meditation is exactly as it sounds—walking around mindfully. This is a type of meditation that has been practiced for thousands of years and has helped many. You might be familiar with Tai Chi, which combines martial arts with the calming properties of meditation. This slow movement centers you and teaches you a lot of self-discipline. During the Golden Age of Zen, walking meditation was the most common type of meditation practiced in China. They believed if you were walking, you might as well be doing it mindfully. Because it is an everyday habit, it becomes easy to incorporate into your life and routines.

Think about how much you walk on an average day. Even if you are not walking to exercise, you still walk from your bed to your kitchen. You walk from your car to your office. There are times where you might walk for an hour in the grocery store. Think about how many opportunities there are for you to transform this time into something meaningful. It is thought that walking meditation becomes a way to bring the idea of mindfulness from meditation into your everyday life. Even if you have never meditated before, walking meditation is suitable for beginners. It provides you with a sense of well-being, and this will allow you to feel grounded as you move about your day.

Below are three ways you can practice walking meditation in your life:

Counting Your Steps

1. Start by walking at a naturally slow place. Try not to overthink the speed of your steps.

2. Keep your posture straight; bring your hands to your diaphragm. This area is located below your lungs. With your left hand up against your diaphragm and your right in front of it, allow your thumbs to cross. Place your left thumb in front of your right. Keep your forearms parallel to the ground.

3. Keep your breathing natural, and pay attention to how many steps you take per breath. You might take three steps per in-breath and four per out-breath. It is common for your inhalations to be shorter.

4. Once you become familiar with your breath pattern, steadily count your steps as you walk.

5. Be mindful as you walk and count. Make it your purpose to pay attention to this and only this.

6. You might notice certain thoughts and sensations rising to the surface as you walk. There might also be some outside distractions that capture your attention. Instead of judging them, simply acknowledge that you notice them and move on. Shift your focus back to your breath, and get back to your counting.

Following Your Steps

1. Start by walking at a naturally slow pace.

2. Just like the prior meditation, place your hands on your diaphragm with your thumbs crossed and arms parallel to the ground.

3. Match your steps to your breath, identifying how many you take per in-breath and per out-breath.

4. Follow the movement of your left foot as you pick it up, swing your leg, and walk forward. Do the same with your right foot. Think about how these three movements create a step.

5. Be mindful as you count your breaths while taking steps.

6. Much like before, your mind might wander and notice certain things. Let this happen as

it wants to, returning back to your focused state once the thought passes through.

Simply Walking

1. Any time you are walking in your daily life, be mindful.
2. Pay attention to what you are doing while you acknowledge what is going on around you. When you are more purposeful, you will feel centered.
3. Dedicate some time each day to your walking meditation practice. With consistency comes results.

Walking meditation is so simple that you might think it sounds too easy—that is because it can be easy if you have the right mindset. This is a simple practice that can provide great benefits for your life. When you are centered, your whole life experience will feel better and more fulfilling. The challenges you face will no longer derail you but, instead, help you seek valuable solutions.

Breath Meditation

Practicing breath meditation is super helpful because it allows you to reduce your stress, anxiety, and tension. There are many things in life that will stress you out, but this does not mean you must take on these burdens daily. Practicing breath meditation is a nice way to allow yourself to let it all go. By getting into the practice of regular meditation, you will be able to work on controlling your temper and sharpening your focus. The things that once bothered you greatly won't seem as bad anymore.

Tell yourself that you are going to commit 15 minutes each day to breath meditation for at least a week. It is thought that your mindfulness will increase the more that you practice. By the end of your first week, you will likely want to continue with your practice because you will notice how much improvement you have already made. Mindful breathing is one of the easiest ways to get used to breathing meditation. This method is as it sounds, and it revolves around your ability to focus on your own breathing.

Your breathing can tell you a lot about what you are feeling. When you are nervous or anxious, your breaths become shallow and sporadic. Without a steady, deep flow of oxygen to your mind and body, this can cause mental and physical problems to arise. While they might come on slowly, they still impact you without you even realizing it. Your thoughts become delayed, or clouded by other thoughts and emotions. You might feel sluggish, unable to harness the proper energy needed for getting through your day.

The following is a basic way for you to get started with mindful breathing:

- **Find a Relaxed Position**: You can choose to either sit or stand with your back upright. To start, it might be more relaxing for you to sit down. Rest your hands wherever they fall naturally, not paying too much attention to their placement. Place your tongue comfortably on the roof of your mouth to release tension in your face.

- **Notice and Relax Your Body**: Pay attention to the shape of your body and the weight it holds. Without judging yourself and your personal appearance, focus on the sensations you are feeling. Notice any areas of tightness you encounter. Do your best to relax them so your entire body feels calm and peaceful.

- **Tune Into Your Breath**: Notice the natural flow of your breath. You don't need to change anything about the way you are breathing; simply observe how it is happening. Ask yourself where you feel your breath. Is it in your nose, your mouth? It might be deeper, in your abdomen. Sometimes, it can even be in your chest or throat. Notice how one breath begins flawlessly as the previous one ends.

- **Be Kind to Your Mind**: Your mind will likely start to wander during this process. If this happens, remind yourself that it is natural. Notice that you are thinking about other things, and get yourself back on track by tuning back into your breathing.

- **Remain Here for Five to Seven Minutes**: Remain here in silence, setting a timer to inform you when your time is up. You will likely wander several times throughout this process. Be kind to yourself, and gently redirect your thoughts the way you did previously.

- **Check-In with Yourself**: After a few minutes, go back to paying attention to your body. Notice how it feels now as compared to how it felt when you first started. Let yourself relax even more, sinking deeper into the joy of the peaceful feeling you are experiencing. Appreciate that you are taking this time for self-care.

As you can see, this is another simple way for you to become familiarized with the art of mediation. You do not need to go through many complex thoughts and themes to experience the benefits meditation can bring. Most people are under the impression that mediation is more complex than this, becoming hesitant to try it for themselves. However, you can always start with the basics and grow from there.

Your meditation practice does not have to be complex or resemble anyone else's. The great thing about meditation is that it is individualized. You get to meditate for your own improvement, not to impress anyone or prove anything to anyone else. Keep in mind that this is a practice for your well-being. When you see how even an act as simple as breathing can be turned into a daily meditation practice, you will appreciate each breath you take even more.

Heart Coherence

Having heart coherence is the idea that your heart guides your mind and body each day. When this occurs, you are thought to experience great things and achieve more. Not only is your heart physically strong, but it also steers you toward loving and fulfilling situations when you listen to it. Heart coherence can help you achieve better physical, mental, and emotional health. Its benefits are abundant and wonderful. Think of your heart as an intelligent part of your body. It has the ability to perceive and decipher, just like your brain. Having this intelligence can be thought of as having intuitive awareness that comes from within. The HeartMath Institute has uncovered that when your emotions align with your heart, your brain and heart have the chance to operate in synergy.

Your heart is made up of a network of around 40,000 neurons that all function distinctly. They are called sensory neurites, and they directly communicate with your brain. These neurons are the reason why you can think of your heart as "intelligent." If you think about the way your heart works, it is amazing. It can function independently, sensing, processing information, making decisions, and demonstrating a learning memory. You might think that the brain sends out the most information, but it is the other way around—the heart sends your brain more information to process. These signals that your heart uses to communicate can often regulate the way you handle your emotions.

When you think about your heart being a coherent organ, it lives up to this assumption by functioning efficiently in a physiological way. This creates an optimal performance in your body by syncing your nervous, cardiovascular, hormonal, and immune systems. If even one of these systems is out of the ordinary, this can create many physical and mental ailments for you. Keeping your heart healthy is important if you want to maintain this optimal health that many strive for. You feel great when you can tell your body is working together as a unit.

When you feel certain emotions, your heart makes sure you feel them physically, too. For example, if you are in a situation that makes you scared, your heart rate will speed up. Many even feel as though their heart is beating in their throats. This is a clear indication that your heart responds to the emotions you feel. However, the rhythmic activity of your heart can also impact your emotions. If your heart rate picks up, this can cause your heart to send signals to your brain, which will impact your emotional state of being. Everything is connected.

It is very important to keep your heart as physically healthy as you can. Because a poor diet or lack of sleep can affect your heart rate, you will also experience a change in your mood and emotions. If you routinely disregard your physical health, this will enforce a negative pattern that will cause your heart to tell your brain that it is unhappy. If you've ever been stuck in a negative mindset, you know how terrible it can feel to be in a bad mood and not understand how to move on from it. The more you settle into these patterns, the more hormones your body will release that will keep you feeling down.

As you can gather, maintaining positive emotions will lead to better rhythmic patterns. If you can keep yourself happy and healthy, your heart rate is going to reflect these efforts. This stability will calm the chaos that is often experienced when you take in a lot of negativity and toxicity. Also, notice that you will sleep better and your immune system will be stronger. Overall, there is no reason why you should not make more of an effort to keep your heart healthy. With the huge connection it maintains with your brain, it makes sense that any effort you put in is going to pay off.

To further motivate yourself to achieve heart coherence, take a look at the benefits you will receive:

- Less cortisol (which means less stress and anxiety)
- A boost in your immune system
- The release of DHEA (an anti-aging hormone)
- Enhanced function of your nervous and digestive systems
- Improved quality of sleep
- A boost in energy level
- Enhanced focus and concentration

- Better ability to learn
- An improvement in problem-solving skills

Another benefit that most overlook is the accelerated function of your intuition. This is the gut instinct that you get when you assess a situation. When you are able to use your intuition, you are going to make wiser decisions in all aspects of your life. You have heard the saying "listen to your heart," and it will never feel truer than once you realize how much your intuition can help you. If you've ever thought twice about doing something because you got a bad feeling, or didn't trust someone that came across the wrong way, these are instances in which your intuition has made an appearance. Be sure to remain mindful of it.

Chapter 8:
Tips to Become the Most Efficient Person Who Can Handle Anything

Curiosity is not only a trait found in young children. As an adult, remaining curious about life and what goes on is a great aspect of your personality to explore. If you would like to become well-versed in handling many different situations, this requires a sense of curiosity to explore and learn. In this chapter, you will discover how learning still benefits you on a daily basis. The skills you gain and the information you process can help to make your life feel more fulfilling and efficient. Instead of getting stuck in the same old routines, you will be able to expand on your true purpose.

Being Curious Keeps You Open

After you reach the stage of adolescence, you typically experience a change in the way you see the world. While you have seen and done many things in your life up until this point, there is still so much more to learn. It can be easy to stop asking as many questions as you did when you were a child and just submit to the norms you see around you. When you are curious, this opens your mind. As an adult now, it can be a refreshing change in pace to reclaim your curiosity. This is how you will end up reaching your full potential.

Being Curious Silences Fear

When you have fears, this means you have certain outcomes in mind. Being stuck in a routine way of thinking will lead you to believe that you have fewer options and opportunities. If you try to be more curious, you will realize there are many solutions available that you might not have thought of before. Instead of being certain that you will fail or that something bad will happen, try to approach your life from a curious perspective. Wonder how well you will do or how much you will learn from the experience. When you no longer let fear lead the way, you will be living your life to the fullest.

Being Curious Leads to Innovation

Think of the most creative minds that come to mind. All of these inventions, projects, and theories each stemmed from curiosity. Without it, innovation would not be possible. This feeling is not only reserved for those who plan on changing the world or inventing cures for illnesses—your life can use more innovation, too. When you don't know what else to do, ask yourself questions. Challenge the way you are currently thinking, and wonder if there is anything you can do to make it better. Deviating from your original plan might be necessary to spark that moment of innovation you need.

Being Curious Reveals Opportunities

You should know that there are many different paths you can take in life. At any given moment, you can choose to change the course of your actions. With a curious mind, you will be able to look beyond what you know and what you think you know. There are many potential opportunities that are waiting for you to find them, but you have to be willing to look. Be open to the things that you would normally say no to; this is how you learn and grow.

Principles of Self-Learning

In today's world, self-learning is becoming increasingly popular. The process of selecting a subject, finding valuable resources, and learning something new is widely practiced by many. This self-starting initiative keeps you current in the age of the constant search for knowledge. Traditionally, you learn in school as you grow up. You are put in front of a teacher who will explain concepts to you and test you on them. As you get older, you are made to rely on your own determination to continue the quest for higher education. Becoming great at self-learning isn't easy for everyone, as we all have unique learning styles. To become better at this process, you must practice it often.

- **Set Learning Goals**: Setting goals for yourself will promote productivity. It is one thing to say you want to do something, but creating deadlines will motivate you to make it happen. Commit to your learning goals, focusing on what it takes to see the end result you desire. If you want to learn a new skill, put a timeline on this task, even if it does not require one. This is going to keep you productive. Make sure that it is realistic, as you do not want to set yourself up for failure. With a goal in mind, you will be motivated to work on your new skill each day. The process will become a part of your daily routine.

- **Assess Your Resources**: There are always resources available for you to use when you wish to learn. Whether you decide to research information, buy tools that will help you learn, or invest in something related to productivity that will help you, it is important you know what you are working with. Make sure that you verify the authenticity of your resources, too. When you are self-learning, you need to fact-check the information you come across. This critical thinking and reasoning will save you from wasting your time on knowledge that isn't real. This part requires a keen eye and concentration. It is easy to be fooled by something that appears very engaging but might not be correct.

- **Engage in a Process**: You need to put yourself on a schedule. No matter what you are trying to learn, this process must be efficient, or else you will become distracted very quickly. Try not to leave too many gaps of unused time in-between time that you wish to learn. This will encourage procrastination and leave you feeling disappointed. Think of ways for you to assess your improvements on the topic. Whether you take quizzes, use flashcards, or have conversations on the topic with those who are more experienced, you need to come up with ways to show that you are making progress. This part can require some trial and error, but you will find the right process that works for your learning style.

- **Apply Your Knowledge**: Once you feel confident about what you have learned, it is time to put it to the test. Think of a real-life situation you can become a part of to apply this knowledge. An example would be conversing with someone who speaks Spanish as their first language if you have taught yourself Spanish. This would be a fully-immersive way to put your language skills to the test. This part can seem scary, but it is a great indicator of what you might need to work on and what you have already done a good job with. You won't know until you try. It is a truly gratifying feeling to see your hard work paying off.

- **Collaborate with Others**: When you pick an area you'd like to learn more about, this gives you access to potential new communities of others who have the same interests. Not only does this mean you can engage with new people, but you can also have the potential of bouncing your ideas off of one another. This is an interactive approach to self-learning that has its benefits. When you talk to others who have an interest in the same information, you might discover facts that you did not already know. Maybe the other person can clarify a concept that you have been struggling with. Keep your eye out for like-minded people, and don't be afraid to open the conversation with what it appears you have in common. If they are passionate about the topic, they will let you know.

- **Share Your Knowledge**: The final step of self-learning comes from the way you are able to give back. After you have made the plan, executed it, and learned, you will be in a position to share your knowledge. Teach someone something new. This will feel very gratifying, and it provides you with a way to put your skills to the test in a new way. Being informed is a great feeling, and it is one that doesn't have to end. As long as you remain curious in your life, you can teach yourself a lot about many different subjects. If you notice another curious person, be patient as you explain to them what you know. Remember that you were also in their position at one point.

Myths of Learning

1. **Re-Reading and Highlighting**: Most people believe that re-reading and highlighting information is essential when studying for tests and processing new

information. According to a study published in the Journal of Psychological Science in the Public, re-reading and highlighting information are both relatively ineffective strategies for retaining information. If your brain is passive during either of these processes, you are not any more likely to remember what you have learned.

2. **Being Right-Brained or Left-Brained**: You have likely heard the comparison before—right-brained people are creative, while left-brained people are logical. A study done in 2013 on the topic revealed something different, however. Scientists from the University of Utah studied over 1,000 brains and found no solid evidence that people use either side of their brains preferentially. While certain basic functions are more dependent on one region than the other, it was proven unlikely that people live their lives solely using one side of their brain versus the other.

3. **The 10,000 Hour Rule**: Made popular by journalist Malcolm Gladwell, this rule states that 10,000 hours of study on any topic is enough to make you a master in the given field. While practice is essential if you want to become great at anything, follow-up studies have been done that show there is no magic number when it comes to the amount of time you spend learning about something.

You need to listen to your own instincts when it comes to how much studying you must do. Certain topics will be picked up quickly, while others will require years to master. With something so subjective, it is impossible to predict when you will finally be an "expert" on the topic.

4. **Sticking with Your First Answer**: On the subject of test-taking, you have probably heard that your first answer is most likely the right answer. Many people second-guess themselves due to nerves while taking tests. Changing answers becomes common as you question if you are on the right track. A study done on college students found that 75% of college students believed in this theory. Reviews on the study, and others like it, showcased that people who change their answers during tests score higher than those who stick with their initial responses. If you feel that you are doubting one of your answers, don't be afraid to revisit it. Sometimes, coming back to it at the end can be enough to see it in a different light.

5. **Intelligence Is Fixed at Birth**: We are all born with natural abilities and talents. Some of us can effortlessly learn how to read music, while others excel at language comprehension. However, your IQ can increase over time. Thanks to what you learn, you can make improvements to your initial

intelligence. Just because you weren't born knowing how to do something does not mean you will never be able to learn. If you have a growth mindset, anything is possible. This type of mindset allows you to hold the belief that there are many opportunities for you in your life. Instead of seeing your choices as fixed decisions, you will learn how to explore all of your options.

6. **Praising Intelligence Is Enough to Motivate Students**: Stanford psychologist Carol Dweck found that telling students they are smart or good at something too frequently can become counterproductive. This type of praise discourages people from taking risks. Without any risks being taken, there is little opportunity for growth or improvement. Dweck states that praising effort or persistence is a much better way to compliment a student. While it is still validating, it gives them the idea that they can do even more. It is important to encourage others to keep working hard and to keep trying, even if they have already achieved some success. Instead of being afraid to make mistakes, they will take this as an opportunity to expand on their knowledge.

7. **We Only Use 10% of Our Brain**: This is a myth that shocks a lot of people, but it is just that—untrue. A widespread myth that has

been used for motivational purposes, this is actually just a misquote taken from a Harvard Professor in the popular self-help book *How to Win Friends and Influence People*. While it is unclear exactly how much of our brain we use on a regular basis, there are no certain limits on our potential. There are plenty of ways in which neuroscience has backed learning that shows we can retain a lot more information and become even more efficient.

8. **There Are Shortcuts to Better Learning**: We all want shortcuts and helpful hints that will accelerate our efforts. When it comes to learning, you must understand that there are no fool-proof ways to study less and retain more. Knowledge requires patience and effort. You must be willing to put in the work if you want to see your desired results. When you take shortcuts, you are only temporarily retaining information. It might seem like you are working on the process more quickly, but you will forget this information over time. Your goal should be to learn in a quality manner, not a speedy manner.

The Learning Success Pyramid

No matter what you do in life, modeling your behavior after a set of proven steps will get you one step closer to success. The next time you aim to reach one of your goals or accomplish a task, consider abiding by the rules of the learning success pyramid. These steps are easily applicable, no matter what must be done. They consistently prove to be worthwhile because they are easy to follow and simple. Unlike other learning pyramids, there are only three steps in the learning success pyramid. By focusing on each one, you will be much happier with your results than if you were to try to split your time between too many steps. The basic model can be seen below.

Step 1—Confidence

How you see yourself is the main foundation of the pyramid. It serves as a base for your actions and behaviors. Without confidence, you will not believe in yourself, even if you are a resilient person. Support from others feels great, but it means nothing if you do not have the necessary confidence to take actionable steps toward learning and accomplishment. The trick to gaining confidence is to know when and how to handle your emotions. You might get wrapped up in negative thoughts that tell you that you aren't good enough or smart enough. Be sure to address these thoughts so you can move on from them, preventing them from impacting your success.

These negative thoughts will enter your mind during the times when you need the most focus. A natural distraction, they can ruin your hard work very easily if you aren't careful. When you notice that you are experiencing a lot of negativity, you need to take action. Make a change that benefits you and your emotional health. Talk about your feelings with someone you trust, write them down, or find an artistic way to express them. As long as they aren't in the foreground of your brain, you should be able to address them and move forward from them. Remind yourself of what you are great at. You have talents that others do not possess, and that makes you special. It is not selfish to own these skills.

Step 2—Self-Management

This step makes up the middle tier of the pyramid. It involves your ability to interact with other people and present yourself how you wish to be perceived. To self-manage, you need to have a lot of discipline and a clear idea of who you are and what you believe in. To best communicate with other people, you need to be organized and ready to face questions. Understand that you need to have the flexibility to realize you are wrong sometimes. Those who are open to learning and growing are naturally better at self-management than those who refuse to change their ways. To truly become great at self-management, you should aim to work on your organization skills. When you can organize your behaviors, this shows others that you are great at completing tasks and holding on to your attention to detail.

Stanford Research Institute did a study that revealed 75% of long-term job success highly depends on your self-management skills. Employers want you to be able to guide yourself and know that you will be making the right decisions, even without their direction. This skill allows employees to be trustworthy and capable. When taking your own initiative, confidence is very important. This is why it is the foundation of the pyramid, with self-management coming in second. The second part of the study revealed that having technical skills only makes up 25% of your job success rate. This shows that you can be well-versed in nearly any subject, but it is your execution of implementing the information that matters most.

Step 3—Learning

Stripping down the definition of learning might help you to accomplish the final step of the pyramid. When you think about it, the art of learning is merely the art of making connections. You are given large amounts of information, and you must determine what you hold on to and what you disregard. With the information you keep, you can then connect it to any past knowledge you have. If the concept is entirely new, simplify it. Break down its steps and see how this information applies to your situation. This type of comparison can be beneficial when learning something new. It can show you that you might already have some kind of familiarity with the concept or with something similar.

The very basic concept of learning relies on your ability to categorize the information you are given. When you expand your knowledge base, you are giving yourself even more chances to make connections. As things start to come together and make sense, you will feel a sense of pride wash over you. It doesn't necessarily take years of study to learn a concept. These tend to come easily if you take the time to break them down. Becoming a master of the subject is what takes time. Much like anything else, practice will improve your learning abilities.

The end... almost!

Reviews are not easy to come by.

As an independent author with a tiny marketing budget, I rely on readers, like you, to leave a short review on Amazon.

Even if it's just a sentence or two!

So if you enjoyed the book, please...

I am very appreciative for your review as it truly makes a difference.

Thank you from the bottom of my heart for purchasing this book and reading it to the end.

Chapter 9:
Learning - Practical Guidelines

The final chapter of this book takes an extended look at learning and what it entails. No matter what you want to learn, you must be able to focus on your goal. You need to have enough passion for the subject to be able to see the benefits of learning more about it. In today's society, it can be hard to stay focused. Even if you generally enjoy the art of learning, there are many distractions that can interrupt the learning process. To avoid them, it is best to increase your attention span. This is the intuition that tells you how long you must stay focused. It promotes the use of your resilient tendencies. If you have a short attention span, this does not mean you are doomed—many of us do. Thanks to handheld electronics, intrusive advertising, and a constant social conversation, it can be hard to know how to tune everything out. There are a few concentration exercises you can rely on. Once you start doing them, your focus will improve and you will be better able to learn when you want to learn.

To get started, make sure you are somewhere where you can be alone and uninterrupted. It would be counterproductive to try these exercises in a busy room or a loud public space. Take this time for yourself and value it. Pick a place to sit where you can be comfortable while maintaining a good posture. Before you begin, take a few calming breaths. Direct your attention to your body and try to relax all of the tense spots. This process of relaxing your muscles from head to toe might feel like meditation. Once you feel relaxed, get into the first exercise. Start by devoting five minutes of your time to it. After the first week, you can increase this to 10 minutes.

Work on one exercise at a time, ensuring you are fully understanding its concept and remembering its details. While you might want to jump ahead and do all of them in one sitting, this is only going to create more noise in your brain. Become great at one before moving on. You might find that you cannot focus some days, and that is frustrating. Don't take it out on yourself—this happens sometimes. This is the point of you trying to work on your concentration. You must be patient with yourself, and give yourself credit for even trying in the first place. Do not set a strict deadline for yourself for this process. Know that you can take as little or as long as you need.

Exercise 1

Pick up any book and count the words in a random paragraph. Once you finish, re-count them to make sure you are correct.

Once you feel like doing this with one paragraph becomes easy, you can do it with two paragraphs each time you complete the exercise. Try to count mentally, and avoid using your finger to count the words.

Exercise 2

Count backward in your mind. Start from 100, and work your way all the way down to zero.

Exercise 3

This is another counting exercise that starts similarly to the above. This time, you will skip three numbers. For example: 100, 97, 94, etc...

Exercise 4

Choose one word to focus on. This can be an inspiring word, something that is on your mind, or something you have read recently. For the duration of the exercise, simply repeat the word silently in your head without letting your thoughts drift.

Exercise 5

Start by looking at a piece of fruit. Give yourself about two minutes to examine it. Make sure you hold it in your hands to verify all of its physical details further. Staying focused on the fruit, set aside any other thoughts that rise to the surface such as where you got the fruit or how much it cost.

After this, close your eyes. Using your imagination, try to use all of your senses (minus sight) to experience the fruit. Imagine how it feels, how it tastes. Only relying on your prior observation, visualize the fruit clearly in your mind.

Methods to Absorb Information Quickly and Easily

- **Transform and Synthesize**: When you are given new information, know that you do not need to hold on to all of it to absorb it. There are many details that you can probably go without holding on to as an effort to make space in your mind for what is important. Work on asking yourself to identify the facts. No matter what the subject is, sift through the information you are given and determine if it is factual and helpful to you learning about it. If there are any opinionated statements thrown in, you might lose track of your goal by putting too much focus on them.

  You must learn how to differentiate between what is necessary and what is unhelpful. Practice this by questioning everything. If you receive an inkling that you are being given too much information to process, explore this thought. Ask yourself why it is too overwhelming and what you can get rid of to make more room. When you keep things simple, you will find the learning experience to be a lot more enjoyable.

- **Combine the New and the Familiar**: As mentioned above, you can use past knowledge that you have to work on remembering new information. If you are presented with a concept that reminds you of something you have already learned or experienced, explore this by asking yourself how the two are connected. Do they follow some of the same principles? Are they indirectly related through another factor? Determine why something is familiar and you might save yourself a lot of work in understanding the information. This process requires keen attention to detail and a lot of patience.

Once you have a good grasp on the new information, explore older concepts again. Ask yourself if you can think of anything that can relate to what you have just learned. By trying to merge ideas again, you are solidifying the new information so you do not forget about it. Making a memory last requires giving yourself a reason to remember it. Is it important? Will it help you in life? Be critical of why you are taking on new information, and you will likely be able to weed out the things that are unnecessary or negative.

- **Self-Testing and Retrieval**: Once you feel that you have mastered a concept, this does not mean the learning experience is over. One of the most effective ways to see what you have learned is by testing yourself. While this does not always mean taking a quiz on the subject matter, you should place yourself in positions where you could potentially use this new information. For example, if you have taught yourself Spanish in your free time, you can put this to the test by conversing with someone in Spanish. Try to speak with someone who uses Spanish as their native language. Reading about it on paper is one thing, but holding a conversation will present you with new challenges.

When you test yourself, this allows you to rely on your memory retrieval. In the example above, you might be struggling to remember how to say a particular word in Spanish. Your mind must think back on all of the lessons you gave yourself, figuring out if it can recall the word you need to remember. You will likely have memories of the methods of learning that you chose. Whether you have a photographic memory and you can remember how the word is spelled, or you use a mnemonic device to remember it. This self-test activates a necessary process of retrieval that will help you become proficient in the information you have learned.

- **Space for Absorption**: After you have learned the information and tested yourself a few times, give yourself some space to absorb all of the concepts. There is no need to keep drilling material that you seem to already know. This is only going to stress you out, which might end up causing you to forget crucial points. Your brain needs some time to breathe when you load a lot of new information into it. Be respectful of this by choosing to do something that will relax your mind. Focus on activities that are peaceful and low-key. You don't need to replace a rigorous task with another one.

You will be amazed at what a good recharging session can do for your brain. When you wake up the next morning, your newly learned information might be clearer to you than ever. By allowing yourself the chance to decompress, you won't have to worry about repeating lessons because all of the important details will still be there. Those who don't let themselves rest often end up doing more work because of this. Work smarter, not necessarily harder.

- **Reading Faster to Retain More**: The speed that you read matters a great deal. Some believe that you retain more when you read slowly, but have you ever tried to speed up the rate in which you read the information? You must be reasonable with your speed, but reading faster might actually end up triggering a very helpful response in your brain. Because the information is passing by more rapidly, your brain will choose things to focus on that are abbreviated but will allow you to still absorb what you are reading. When you can get through the content faster, there is also less room for you to become distracted.

Put this theory to the test by picking up a book that you have never read before. Increase your reading speed, finishing the book sooner than you would if you read it normally. After, write down the main plot points, important information, and highlights that you can remember. If you cannot recall all of the details at first, that is okay. The point is that you have the foundation in your memory, and writing these points down might lead you to recall other supporting information.

- **Changing Locations**: Your environment makes a big difference in your ability to learn. As you know, distractions are already all around you. They can come in physical forms, such as people walking into the room. They can also come in the form of intrusive thoughts or noises in the distance. Give yourself a change of scenery and see how much this impacts your ability to absorb information better. If you normally work from your bed, try moving to your kitchen table. Checking your emails in this environment might prove to be helpful because you will be able to focus on them better. It is always a good idea to work where you do not rest because your brain will already have a strong association with the latter.

You can also make a bigger change, like going to a library to learn, for instance. Getting out of your familiar environment entirely can help you focus a lot better. When you have many pieces of information to sort through, giving yourself space away from familiarity might be one of the best ways to truly absorb everything. Understand that you can change your environment as much as you need to. If you cannot control it at home, then you can move to a different location for the purpose of better learning.

How to Combine Long-Term and Short-Term Memories

Your brain is incredibly powerful. It has what is equivalent to 2.5 million gigabytes of memory storage. Putting this into perspective—you can hold up to three million hours of television shows! While there is a lot of power behind your memory, you must learn how to use it correctly if you want to take advantage of all this space. On an average day, you learn many new things, but it is up to your long-term memory to turn this into something that sticks. Normally, your short-term memory will absorb the information, only to let it go later on. To better understand how your memory works, it is important to understand its components.

Sensory Register

When you use your senses to take in information, your brain holds on to it for a few seconds. What your brain deems important is what gets permanently input into your sensory register. For example, specific people are normally committed to your memory permanently.

You can take control of this process by telling your brain that you want to commit certain information to memory. Imagine you are driving and looking for the right exit to take. You know that it is exit number 173, so you pay close attention to the road signs. Your sensory register is going to see all of the preceding sign numbers, but you don't necessarily need to commit all of them to your memory. Concentrate most on exit 173, and think of the others as components of this tidbit of knowledge.

Short-Term Memory

This branch of memory deals with what is known as your working memory. This becomes an essential part of your memory-storing process because this is the point where your brain decides how to work with the information. At this point, you will have the most control to do with the information as you wish.

Using the example above, you should tell your brain that exit 173 is the most important because that is the exit you need to take. While you should not forget about exits 172, 171, and 170, they are arguably less important in this case. You can commit them to your short-term memory, only to exist at the moment. When you use them for context, you will be able to remember better which exit you are going to take.

While you might want to remember the exit you took for the future, you do not have to commit the rest of them to your long-term memory. This is a way for you to sort through the information and only hold on to what is necessary. It is a very helpful and streamlined process that will keep you focused.

Long-Term Memory

Imagine you were given a phone number to memorize. To commit it to your short-term memory, you repeated it to yourself over and over again until you were able to write it down. Now, that phone number is likely stored in your long-term memory or at least part of it. You can make it a permanent fixture in your mind by refreshing yourself on the information. Because you took proactive steps to tell your brain that it needed to be committed to your short-term memory, you were able to hold on to it for long enough to make it permanent.

As you can see, combining your short-term memory and your long-term memory is an essential part of memorization as a whole. There are a few ways to practice this when you must hold on to something that you do not want to forget.

1. **Method of Loci**: "Loci" means "places" in Latin. This is a strategy that dates back to ancient Roman and Grecian times. Start by visualizing a space you are very familiar with.

This can be your house or your workplace. Make sure you pick somewhere that allows you to recall many details.

Think about each room, hallway, and turn. Now, imagine that you place an item that you want to remember in a specific location in the space. This doesn't have to be a material item. It can be a concept, such as a phone number.

When you need to recall the item, think about the room you left it in. Visualize the space, paying close attention to everything that you can remember about it. Go through the room in your mind, and repeat the exercise as much as necessary.

2. **Peg System**: There is an alternative to the above method. This one requires you to use mnemonic skills to help your memory. To use this system, you will associate specific words with a series of numbers they represent. This will create little "pegs" that you can hang pieces of information from. Using nouns and numbers between one and 10 typically works best. It is also incredibly helpful to rhyme the word with the number.

Make a list of important items you need to remember. Mentally hang a picture of the first item on peg number one. Continue adding items, one piece at a time to the next peg in the series. Once you have all of them hanging from your pegs, review them in order.

Once they are organized in front of you, then you should be able to create your mnemonic devices to help you remember the information. This system is great because it encourages you to organize your thoughts from the very beginning.

3. **The Major System**: This is a memory technique designed to help you remember long series of numbers. The system helps you create words out of number pairs. To get started, you can take the phone number example into consideration again. Imagine the number you must remember is 535-867-5309.

Reformat this number by sorting it into pairs. It should now read: 53-58-67-53-09.

Using the below table, you can turn your pairs into consonant sounds to help you remember the phone number.

Zero: Associated letters are z, s, and soft z
One: Associated letters are t, d, and th
Two: Associated letter is n
Three: Associated letter is m

Four: Associated letter is r
Five: Associated letter is l
Six: Associated letters are ch, soft g, j, sh, c, and s
Seven: Associated letters are k, hard c, ch, q, and hard g
Eight: Associated letters are f, v, ph, and gh
Nine: Associated letters are p and b

Taking the phone number and using this table, you can come to realize that the words you can use to remember it are lamb (5-3), live (5-8), shock (6-7), limb (5-3), and sob (0-9). Now, create a story using the words you were given.

"The lamb was lucky enough to live through a terrible electric shock. It had a hurt limb, which caused it to sob."

Now, work backward by reciting your story, thinking about each individual word associated with the number pairs, and recall the phone number.

Conclusion

You have many opportunities, as long as you are willing to seek them. Through the process of personal transformation, you will understand how to select better habits that will benefit your life. Instead of using distractions and other methods to keep yourself from being productive, you will have a renewed passion for your life and a newfound love for yourself. Being a well-rounded person is a lot more than being smart or efficient. While this becomes a part of it, you must also be happy with who you are and clear about what you represent. There are many aspects of today's society that want you to conform to what everyone else is doing, but know that you can choose your own path.

To best summarize the information you have learned, make sure you remember these key points:

- Improving yourself involves letting go of your past. If you are still holding on to negativity that happened a long time ago or worrying about a past choice you made, this must be addressed before you can move on. Work through the emotions that hold you back, and identify what you must do to get the closure you deserve.

- Change the way you see yourself by reminding yourself that you have changed a lot over the last few years. You have your own set of beliefs, interests, and a unique personality. Learn how to appreciate these things, as they make up who you are.

- Emotions can do a lot more than cloud your headspace. Negative emotions can actually impact you physically, too. Depending on what you are dealing with, you might experience such things as digestive problems, headaches, or even heart attacks. This is yet another reason why it is important to address your emotional wellness on a regular basis.

- You need to take action as soon as possible if you want to experience a positive personal transformation. The opportunities are not going to wait around for you. Most of the time, actionable steps are required if you plan on making progress. Tell yourself that now is the best time to take action. Imagine how much you can change your life.

- To be productive, you must eliminate distractions. They will only cause you to procrastinate and make you feel bad about not getting enough done. When you work on your skills in the right environment, you will be met with the successful outcome that you desire.

- Appreciate who you are as a person without comparing yourself to others around you. There is a difference between comparison to tear yourself down and comparison to feel inspired. Assess if the comparisons you have been making are helping you or hurting you.

- Gratitude is very important. When you can feel thankful for what you already have and learn how to be kind to others, you will have a newfound appreciation for your life. Volunteer your time and get out of your comfort zone; this will help you.

- Practice the art of unbiased thinking. Know that past experiences you've had can influence whether or not you have biases. As you listen to others talk, make sure you are listening to hear them rather than to respond or make assumptions.

- Meditation is a great way to reset your mind. This is necessary if you want to take a more positive approach to your life. You will have the chance to clear your head while relaxing your body. This combination proves to be successful.

- Curiosity will make you smarter. When you have the desire to learn new information, this is one way to keep your brain active and healthy. The more ideas you are open to receiving, the more you will be able to formulate in-depth opinions. This makes you a well-rounded person.

- When you are able to set your focus, anything is possible. There are many techniques and tips outlined in this book to help you do just that. Use them at any time to create positive habits that will help you throughout the rest of your life.

As promised, you have the ability to change your own life, as long as you are willing to work hard at it. Once you practice these tips, you will learn how to get rid of the things that no longer serve you to make room for what is useful. You are going to feel a lot happier and healthier, both mentally and physically. Seeking more from your life is one way to keep you constantly inspired to do better. There are many solutions within this book that you can use to help you along the way.

By building up your confidence, you will see that anything is possible when you put your mind to it. Know that you are a strong person who can make any changes necessary that will benefit your happiness. You do not have to live with constant uncertainty and stress. Use your curiosity to clear up these issues, and make sure you completely address each one before you move on from it. Getting into this habit will ensure that negative emotions do not build up and hinder you.

Remember that the definition of success is subjective. What might seem abundant to you might not be the same for someone else. You must follow your own path and listen to your own emotions to determine if you are really living your best life. Give yourself credit where credit is due, and know that being flexible will help you overcome additional obstacles along the way. If you fail at first, try again while using a different method. You aren't always going to get it right on the first try because there are so many approaches you can take; this is the point of living a fulfilling life. You must be willing to take risks and make sacrifices for the benefit of your health and happiness.

References

11 Surprising Ways Emotions Can Affect Your Body. (2018, February 16). Retrieved from https://brightside.me/wonder-curiosities/10-emotions-that-have-a-huge-impact-on-your-body-451610/

Belin, A. (2019, September 02). The Importance of Self Improvement No Matter How Old You Are. Retrieved from https://www.lifehack.org/819195/importance-of-self-improvement

Blackman, A. (2018, August 11). What Are Self-Limiting Beliefs? +How to Overcome Them Successfully. Retrieved from https://business.tutsplus.com/tutorials/what-are-self-limiting-beliefs--cms-31607

Brenner, A. (2017, August 23). Six Ways to Focus on What's Important in Your Life. Retrieved from https://www.psychologytoday.com/us/blog/in-flux/201708/six-ways-focus-whats-important-in-your-life

Bundrant, M. (2019, November 25). How to Overcome Limiting Beliefs That Hold You Back from Success. Retrieved from https://www.lifehack.org/articles/productivity/stop-limiting-beliefs-and-take-back-your-life.html

Cleare, L. (2018, October 27). 4 Reasons Why Being A Curious Learner Will Save Your Life.

Retrieved from https://laquitacleare.com/4-reasons-why-being-a-curious-learner-will-save-your-life/

Clément, S. (2020, March 06). Heart Coherence is perhaps the most important thing you need to know. Retrieved from https://www.gaiameditation.com/heart-coherence/

Cole. (2014, July 27). How Top Executives Turn Problems Into Opportunities, And You Can, Too. Retrieved from https://www.fastcompany.com/3033550/how-top-executives-turn-problems-into-opportunities-and-you-can-too

Forte, T. (2020, February 01). How Emotions Are Made: The Theory of Constructed Emotion. Retrieved from https://fortelabs.co/blog/how-emotions-are-made/

Gelles, D. (n.d.). How to Meditate. Retrieved from https://www.nytimes.com/guides/well/how-to-meditate

Heylighten, F. (2006, April 19). The Newtonian World View. Retrieved from http://pespmc1.vub.ac.be/NEWTONWV.html

Ho, L. (2020, March 11). 7 Steps to Make Self-Learning Effective for You. Retrieved from https://www.lifehack.org/853724/self-learning

James, S. (2018, January 13). How To Master Your Emotions: The 6 Steps To Emotional Mastery. Retrieved from https://projectlifemastery.com/control-your-emotions/

Kabat-Zinn, J. (2019, March 21). A Meditation on Observing Thoughts, Non-Judgmentally. Retrieved from https://www.mindful.org/a-meditation-on-observing-thoughts-non-judgmentally/

Kageyama, N. (2017, June 30). "Productive Failure": A Teaching Method Which Leads to Short Term Failure, but Long Term Success. Retrieved from https://bulletproofmusician.com/productive-failure-how-strategic-failure-in-the-short-term-can-lead-to-greater-success-and-learning-down-the-road/

Madill, E. (2019, February 12). Why Breaking Out of the Comparison Trap Can Make Us Happier. Retrieved from https://thriveglobal.com/stories/if-you-want-an-abundant-life-say-goodbye-to-comparison/

Mckee, M. (2006, September 04). Introduction: Quantum World. Retrieved from https://www.newscientist.com/article/dn9930-introduction-quantum-world/

Miller, J. (2016, July 12). 8 Ways To Have More Gratitude Every Day. Retrieved from https://www.forbes.com/sites/womensmedi

a/2016/07/08/8-ways-to-have-more-gratitude-every-day/

O'Donovan, K. (2016, January 17). 4 Reasons Taking Action Is Crucial In Achieving Success. Retrieved from https://addicted2success.com/success-advice/4-reasons-taking-action-is-crucial-in-achieving-success/

O´Donovan, K. (2020, March 31). How To Break the Procrastination Cycle. Retrieved from https://www.lifehack.org/articles/productivity/how-break-the-procrastination-cycle.html

Paul, A. (2014, February 25). The Hidden Benefits Of A 'Productive Failure'. Retrieved from https://www.businessinsider.com/hidden-benefits-of-productive-failure-2014-2?international=true

Proctor, M. (2017, March 21). 6 Science-Backed Ways Being Kind Is Good for Your Health. Retrieved from https://www.quietrev.com/6-science-backed-ways-being-kind-is-good-for-your-health/

Sasson, R. (n.d.). Concentration Exercises for Training and Focusing the Mind. Retrieved from https://www.successconsciousness.com/blog/concentration-mind-power/concentration-exercises/

Stenger, M. (2018, February 15). 10 Common Learning Myths That Might Be Holding You

Back. Retrieved from https://www.opencolleges.edu.au/informed/features/10-common-learning-myths-might-holding-back/

Valentine, M. (2015, December 14). The Beginner's Guide to Walking Meditation. Retrieved from https://buddhaimonia.com/blog/walking-meditation-guide

Vaiana, D. (2020, January 14). How to Improve Your Memory: A Comprehensive, Science-Backed Guide. Retrieved from https://collegeinfogeek.com/how-to-improve-memory/

What Does "Be Present" Actually MEAN, and How Do I Do It?! (2019). Retrieved from https://louisethompson.com/what-does-be-present-actually-mean-and-how-do-i-do-it/

Winston, D. (2018, November 27). A 5-Minute Breathing Meditation To Cultivate Mindfulness. Retrieved from https://www.mindful.org/a-five-minute-breathing-meditation/

Winter, S. (2018, November 23). The Success Pyramid: A Model of Efficient and Effective Learning. Retrieved from https://studyskills.com/educators/the-success-pyramid/

www.ingramcontent.com/pod-product-compliance
Lightning Source LLC
LaVergne TN
LVHW020925090426
835512LV00020B/3214